T0067945

THE LORD, THE LINK, AND THE LOST

THE LINK BAPTIST CHURCH

WESTBOW
PRESS®
A DIVISION OF THOMAS NELSON
& ZONDERVAN

Scripture quotations marked NKJV are taken from the New King James Version®. Copyright © 1982 by Thomas Nelson. Used by permission. All rights reserved.

WestBow Press books may be ordered through booksellers or by contacting:

WestBow Press
A Division of Thomas Nelson & Zondervan
1663 Liberty Drive
Bloomington, IN 47403
www.westbowpress.com
1 (866) 928-1240

ISBN: 978-1-9736-5695-1 (sc)
ISBN: 978-1-9736-5696-8 (e)

Library of Congress Control Number: 2019902974

Print information available on the last page.

WestBow Press rev. date: 03/27/2019

CONTENTS

PREFACE

A major disconnect exists between the generations in the church. It is prevalent among the millennial generation. In a recent prayer meeting with pastors, deacons, laypersons, teachers, and leaders from varied churches and denominations, we prayed about issues in Macon, Georgia—our lovely city and state, the nation, and the world. It was observed that the common focus of prayer was our children and grandchildren—the millennials! We concluded that the common denominator for the missing link in the church is primarily the millennial generation. The Link Baptist Church family felt a need to not only address this situation with the millennials but also that of Generation Z. Thus, we were led in prayer to make a statement particularly to the millennials and generally to Generation Z. This book is evidence of our desire to not only make a difference but to also make a personal appeal, inviting the next generation to church. It is the work of the membership—individually and collectively.

A special thanks to my Geraldine, my wife, for being my buddy, pal, and best friend. I would not be able to do this without her. Pamela Paul, Clem Agee, Twila Gitschalg, Karmin and Bennie Baker, Adrianna Cooper-Jones, Octavious Smith, Aneitra Stephens, Lisa Murphy, Michelle Harper, Kameron Agee, Keishe`a Paul, Angelia Denson, Brittnay Harrell-Stanley, Zachery Stanley, and Timothy Cochran are valuable members of the church who shared their God-given wisdom beyond measure and my mother, Mrs. Ola Finney, who has been a huge blessing. The children: Trinity Carter,

Truth Carter, and Keara Dunn have proven that there are some children who are listening. Their contributions are invaluable. They represent the hope for today and tomorrow. Last, but certainly not least, I would like to thank the members of The Link Baptist Church who sacrificed time away from family for this endeavor. Jesus Christ is Lord and Savior. We dedicate this book: "*The Lord, the Link, and the Lost*" to the furthering of His Kingdom. Thank you, Lord Jesus. We love you so very much.

Until Jesus Returns,
Kenneth H. Mc Millan, DTh

INTRODUCTION

In America--a multi-cultured country--the unchurched are viewing the church to see if it can or will cross racial and cultural lines and unite as one body, worshipping and serving God. They are looking to see if Americans can produce a church that will allow people of the same community to worship together. They are looking to see if the church itself can truly live up to its creed of including all people. Some church members are willing to embrace multiculturalism, and others are not. When the church proclaims the truth of Jesus Christ and display what she proclaims, then and only then can the multicultural movement be effective.

America has been experiencing rapid population changes during the past several years. This trend is expected to continue at an alarming rate into the next millennium, which means that most communities will be multicultural. Churches have also been experiencing rapid population changes as well. Many Christians have stopped attending church, and many non-Christians who have never attended church have no intention of attending. Thus, there is much work to be done by the church. Three significant components are involved in this puzzle: The Lord, The Link, and The Lost, and they are intertwined. Our Lord and Savior, Jesus Christ, left explicit mandates to the church outlining how to tackle these issues.

Chapter 1

THE LORD

It is evident that continuing to spread the Gospel—the Good News—was important to Jesus, our Lord and Savior. He issued the following mandate to His disciples before ascending to Heaven: *"Go therefore and make disciples of all the nations, baptizing them in the name of the Father and of the Son and of the Holy Spirit"* (Matthew 28:19). He had spent a lot of time imparting knowledge to the 12 men He chose to mentor. He counseled, taught, and supported them. As any good mentor would desire for his or her mentee to carry on the process with another mentee and create a chain, the Lord was no exception. In fact, He was the first mentor—the first and greatest teacher—who created the greatest lesson plan! He was not self-centered or selfish; He left His lesson plan with His mentees and insisted that they follow it and pass it on to the next generation so they would be equipped to do likewise. *"And the things that you have heard from me among many witnesses, commit these to faithful men who will be able to teach others also"* (2 Timothy 2:2).

In the teaching/learning process, He expounded and gave examples, ensuring that they understood clearly. He was the model teacher! He varied His teaching methods; He taught in individual, small group, and whole group sessions. He was not just a master teacher; He was *the* master teacher! He had the disciples train directly under Him, as He sent them out to perform certain ministry tasks to ensure they had the skill level and confidence to do what He had done. He was then able to show them what they needed to correct. He wanted to make sure they were ready to carry the torch. As teachers do, He gave them tests. He tested their faith and trust in Him. He told them exactly what they needed to do. *"Most assuredly, I say to you, he who believes in Me, the works that I do he will do also; and greater works than these he will do, because I go to My Father"* (John 14:12).

Before sending them out, the Lord gave the disciples step-by-step instructions telling them exactly where to go and what to do.

These twelve Jesus sent out and commanded them, saying: "Do not go into the way of the Gentiles, and do not enter a city of the Samaritans.

But go rather to the lost sheep of the house of Israel.

And as you go, preach, saying, 'The kingdom of heaven is at hand.'

Heal the sick, cleanse the lepers, raise the dead, cast out demons. Freely you have received, freely give.

Provide neither gold nor silver nor copper in your money belts,

nor bag for your journey, nor two tunics, nor sandals, nor staffs; for a worker is worthy of his food.

Now whatever city or town you enter, inquire who in it is worthy, and stay there till you go out.

And when you go into a household, greet it.

If the household is worthy, let your peace come upon it. But if it is not worthy, let your peace return to you.

And whoever will not receive you nor hear your words, when you depart from that house or city, shake off the dust from your feet. Matthew 10:5-14

He also explained the superior/subordinate relationship between teacher and student. *"A disciple is not above his teacher, but everyone who is perfectly trained will be like his teacher"* (Luke 6:40). He wanted to instill in them that although they would never be greater than the teacher, they would be like their teacher after being fully trained.

Chapter 2

THE LINK

Within the past 60 years, changes have taken place in the workplace, in schools, in communities throughout the United States, and in churches. During this time, America moved from a segregated society to an integrated society in all areas. Surprisingly, within recent years, the trend seems to be shifting back to segregated schools because more parents are pulling their children out of integrated public schools and enrolling them into private, predominately one-race schools. However, society, in general, has not returned to segregation; the communities and the workplace remain integrated. Diversity, however, has transcended the workplace and has entered the worship place. This trend involves churches with declining membership combining with other churches, producing a cross or multicultural effect. It also involves people exercising freedom of choice to attend, visit, or connect with the church of their choice without regard to race.

As society diversifies, local churches find themselves interacting with people from every tribe and tongue, but not every church is equipped to handle the realities of ethnic and racial diversity in their congregational life. They must be willing to do whatever is necessary to fulfill the great commission and to follow the guidelines for establishing churches as outlined in the New Testament of the Holy Bible. Thus, if the church is to be effective, she must follow the examples outlined in the scriptures, which were inspired by Jesus. Churches must rethink the purpose, take an internal look at the institution, come together, and rebuild as God has planned. John writes:

> *After these things I looked, and behold, a great multitude which no one could number, of all nations, tribes, peoples, and tongues, standing before the throne and before the Lamb, clothed with white robes, with palm branches in their hands.* Revelation 7:9

Thus, the true church is multicultural in nature, and churches of today must permit the Holy Spirit to lead and guide in all undertakings. As church leaders rethink the design, makeup, and establishment of the church, many have come to not only view the church as being multicultural in nature but have also acted on making it a reality—just as God planned. This bold movement has positively affected nonbelievers and church members who had stopped or almost stopped attending church services. It has also been a motivational force and has significantly created unity in worship with varied cultures.

Although Jesus exhorts all to love and to follow the dictates of the Holy Spirit, some churches have their own initiatives and programs and only cater to the members of their own congregations. They also only cater to those in need who reside within the church community and who mirror the makeup of the congregation. Churches that fail to understand that the less fortunate can come from any race or culture fail to put love in action and to heed God's command.

The aim of the multicultural church is to unite people across racial and cultural lines. However, if the church is to have an impact on the community, the words of Jesus Christ must be heeded, and a right relationship with the Holy Spirit must be obtained and maintained. The church, established as God planned, should be blind in terms of the race or culture of those in need of assistance. Race or culture should not matter; the Word (James 2:15-17) specifically commands the church to meet the physical needs of the less fortunate.

> *If a brother or sister is naked and destitute of daily food, and one of you says to them, "Depart in peace, be warmed and filled," but you do not give them the things which are needed for the body, what does it profit? Thus also faith by itself, if it does not have works, is dead.*

People will not listen if they do not see love in action. Countless surveys have been conducted and reveal similar reasons why so many people do not attend church. The reasons all center around the worship experience, which should be full of love. People attending worship services want to see and feel love. Love must fill the atmosphere—from the door to the pulpit and choir stand. All worshippers must be made to feel a part of the experience. This is particularly true in multicultural communities where the residents hear more talk and see little to no expressions of love. When they do attend church, they must be well received and made a part of the worship experience. If not, their first visit will probably be their last. Church members must recognize and treat them as their neighbors; after all, that is just what they are. Church members should also heed God's command to love them as they love themselves and value them mainly because they are also made in the image of God.

The true multicultural church is ready to live out her creed to embrace the community as a whole—every man, woman, boy, and girl—regardless of race. To fulfill the mission, the multicultural church must be open to God and acknowledge His grace and mercy. Pastors, other church leaders, and laity must be willing to do what is necessary to fulfill the great commission and to follow the guidelines for establishing churches as outlined in the New Testament. When the church embraces the mercy and grace of

God as the foundation, doors are opened for the people to dialogue, worship, and receive the blessings of God.

Meeting needs has been a mission of the church from the beginning. The church at Antioch cut across the entire social spectrum, from Herod's foster brother to the slave. In addition, the community cut across racial lines (the Jews and the Gentiles) not only in theory but also in practice. When the people at Antioch heard that the Jews had a material need in a different geographical location in Judea, they combined their funds and sent them on a long journey to meet the needs of their brothers. *"Then the disciples, each according to his ability, determined to send relief to the brethren dwelling in Judea"* (Acts 11:29). The multicultural church is committed to meeting the needs of a varied population.

In the traditional church, people selected their place of worship based on principles and denominational ties. Baptists, for example, searched for Baptist churches, and Methodists searched for Methodist churches. Further, Caucasians searched for churches comprised of all or predominately Caucasian members, and Black people searched for churches comprised of all or predominately Black members. That is no longer the case. Times have changed, and people are more concerned about the style of worship and the quality of ministry, and the church must meet this demand. This does not mean evangelism should be thrown out the door and the primary focus placed on the style and quality of ministry. It simply means that the worship experience is extremely important to worshippers. Thus, churches that are not willing to open their doors and embrace the multicultural concept will not grow. The key is to learn how to obtain and maintain a balance, considering the style of worship and the evangelistic experience of all who enter the doors. It is often through evangelism that people visit churches. In many cases they are invited, and in some cases, they are motivated because of an evangelistic encounter with a congregant or a missionary.

A multiethnic worship experience is exciting, but it could potentially be very uncomfortable for various ethnicities and everyone else who may become a participant. Understanding various cultures is not easy, but it is not impossible. General observations reveal difficulties in getting people to worship together. This has been a major challenge because of diverse cultures and backgrounds. It appears that people do not want to learn about people of different ethnicities or how they live. To have an effective multicultural and diversified church, we must be willing to communicate and listen to one another. Communication is key because the dialogue must start somewhere. Listening to others and learning about their background is very important. Making an honest attempt to sit down and fellowship during a meal with people from different cultural backgrounds can increase one's knowledge and possibly change one's views of an entire race. God seems to do something supernatural when we make a concerted effort to commune over a meal with people who do not look or act like us.

For the church to reach people of diverse cultures, church leaders and congregants must be willing to come out of their comfort zones and love others enough to admit limited or no knowledge about their culture or ethnicity. When the love of God dwells in us, we will be compelled to make a difference. That difference can be made when we reach out to others of different cultures and ethnicities. We must put fear and ignorance to the side and give the peace and love of God a chance. The world is waiting to hear the sweet sound and message of Jesus Christ.

Statistics

According to a 2018 report from Baylor University, a comparison of multiracial congregations in the United States in 1998 and 2012 revealed multiracial congregations increased from 6% in 1998 to 12% in 2012. Five percent more Americans worshipped in multiracial congregations in 2012 than in 1998--from 13% in 1998 to 18% in 2012. Catholic churches remained ahead of

Protestant and Evangelical Protestant churches in terms of the number of multiracial congregations. The number of Black clergy head ministers in multiracial congregations increased 12%, from 5% in 1998 to 17% in 2012. In the past, Latinos were considered the most likely to worship with Caucasians; however, Blacks have replaced them. Approximately 25% of Blacks comprised multiracial congregations across America in 2012, a 9% increase from 16% in 1998. Multiracial churches, however, experienced a 9% decrease in Latino attendance. A decrease of approximately 2% was experienced by multiracial congregations in immigrant attendance.

Developing Diversity and Unity

Listed below are some beliefs and qualities church leaders and members must possess to develop diversity and unity.

1. Believe that there must be *total* dependency on God.
2. Believe that there must be *honesty* in *all* things.
3. Believe that the church must be *relevant* and *cultured*.
4. Believe that relationships must be *authentic*.
5. Believe that all believers must be *empowered*.
6. Believe that church congregants and/or members must be *diverse*.
7. Trust that the Lord Jesus Christ *leads* and *inspires* leaders to make a difference in the world.
8. Live out *core values* that have defined the new age multicultural church.
9. Have a spirit of *unity* to come together and make a difference.
10. Have a mission of *going* despite impending challenges or obstacles.

The Role of the Pastor and Church Leaders

Pastors are key in the building of a multicultural church and in evangelizing to the unsaved and the unchurched. They must not only set the tone; they must lead in the decision-making process regarding making the worship experience meaningful for all worshippers—regardless of race or culture. They must be change agents and be able to lead their congregations into change for the better of all who enter the doors of the church. They must allow the Holy Spirit to lead in the building of the church across racial and cultural lines. They must also be knowledgeable of the characteristics of a growing church in relation to the worship service, which includes everything from the physical environment and the sermon to the invitation to discipleship. In addition, they must be knowledgeable of the needs and the racial/cultural makeup of the church community and initiate a plan of action to meet the needs. Most importantly, they must be willing to, with the assistance of other church leaders, redesign the entire structure of worship under the guidance of the Holy Spirit.

The Biblical principles that have been set before us in the New as well as the Old Testament writings must be followed to the letter. For the church of today to be effective in reaching the people, the undeniable Word of God must be the power source. This approach within itself leads one to be totally dependent on the fact that the Spirit of God must be equal in value to the Word of God. Not only should church leaders develop ideas and plans, taking into consideration what looks and sounds good, they must not forget that the desired results can and only will be accomplished by listening to the Spirit of God and being directed by God Himself.

Just as school administrators are the instructional leaders in schools, pastors are the key leaders in the church. Pastors must recapture the New Testament design in terms of influencing lives through their witness. They must assess what the church is doing for the good of the church community and determine if the church has any influence in the community at large. If so, they must determine its impact (Lewis and Wilkins, 2001). After determining the impact, they must determine if the impact is positive.

Church leaders must understand that major changes in structure are needed to prepare, assist, and send people into areas of service in which they feel they have been called. Structure, not preaching, is the way to achieve the influence that is needed in proving to the world that the truth it proclaims is worth considering. Church leaders who are serious about developing the congregants and connecting to the church community will quickly realize that the church structure must be revamped (Lewis & Wilkins, 2001).

According to a 2018 Baylor University study, former research reveals that congregations have embraced varied techniques to promote racial diversity. Some techniques include integrating various types of music, incorporating more engagement during worship, accommodating small groups to promote multiethnic systems, and constructing plans to address issues regarding ethnicity. The study also revealed that newly established churches or churches with shorter histories are more apt to embrace diversity, while it is more difficult for churches with long histories to embrace diversity. With this revelation, as a move toward embracing diversity and making the church atmosphere more inviting for worshippers of all ethnicities, a significant number of younger congregants of churches with long traditional histories may be needed to bring the topic of diversity before the church.

In building the multicultural church, a plan of action is needed and should include selecting, motivating, preparing, and empowering prospective church leaders to join the bandwagon in fulfilling the Great Commission. The Lord gave us the great commission to go out into the world to seek and save the lost. Leaders and believers who heed the call must have a deep-seated hope of reaching the lost.

How one acts within the family setting is often the way he or she acts outside the family setting. When Christianity is exhibited within the home, it is usually exhibited within the church, which is a blessing. When we lead at home and in the church, we are ready to go into the world and seek the lost. It originates in the home and is supplemental to the church.

Church leaders must know that quality impacts church growth. It matters in every area of life, from service provided in restaurants to the worship experience in churches. It all begins with the key leader in the church—the pastor. If pastors are committed to lead as Jesus led, they will be the initiators in building bridges in cross-cultural partnerships. They must step up to the plate and build relationships between churches and within the church community to bring about reconciliation in worship experiences and community involvement.

As aforementioned, a plan of action is necessary. Determining the needs and desires of the church community is paramount. Sadly, some church leaders in established churches have never conducted research *on* their church community; neither have they conducted research *within* their church community. Therefore, these church leaders cannot compare research from previous years to determine progress. In such cases, the worship services and activities are planned with no thought of what the community needs or what the community desires. Church leaders who review previously conducted community research are positioning to help the church community. The information obtained would help church leaders become more knowledgeable of how to build the church. The research would be beneficial in documenting the racial makeup of the community. It would also aid church leaders in determining the needs and desires of the varied cultures, which would in turn aid them in preparing varied worship experiences for the targeted group.

The collected information should be compared with the prioritized list of needs to determine if the churches are synchronized with the real needs of the community. The findings would dispel any incorrect assumptions. The survey would also document major issues in addition to those the church leaders conducted of their individual church communities. It takes the guesswork out of the project and presents the facts. Most importantly, it would point to the needs—the prime targets for ministry.

Reviewing survey results is just one step in the process. In terms of functioning, the church cannot remain where it is because God ordained it to function differently. Segregation is a major issue in the city in which the multicultural church referenced in this book is located. The sense of unity among believers of different ethnicities is lacking; the Anglo churches worship together, and the Black churches worship together. Because the Lord is the God of unity, operating in this manner must break His heart.

Reconciliation is desperately needed; however, to converse about reconciliation, we must be willing to have open dialogue about the separation. We must come together in truth and honesty in a spirit of prayer. When leaders bring the Holy Spirit into the conversation, God provides a true sense of direction. It is, however, very difficult to preach and teach on cross-cultural ministry to people who are not willing to come out of their comfort zones and deal with it directly.

Pastors of growing churches and those who are embracing multiculturalism must make sure their sermons are biblically based, relevant, interesting, entertaining, simple, encouraging, and positive. This is true for pastors of any church. It is significant to note that pastors who are about serving the present age must resolve to do more regarding serving the church members and guests the Word of God. They must increase their study time as well as their meditation time. They must make more time to listen to God as He speaks to them on how and what to deliver to His people. They must take the business of preaching even more seriously as they reach out to people of various nationalities or to those that they may have never imagined would enter the church doors.

Church leaders—pastors in particular—must be very sensitive to the preferences of the targeted group. They cannot, however, be sensitive or compassionate if they have not attempted to discover their preferences. Knowing the preferences is especially important because the church leaders and laity invite the unchurched to worship services or to church activities. It is, however, very important that church leaders and laity realize that not all unchurched people are unsaved. They may have simply become disenchanted or bored with worship as usual. This is one reason their preferences must be considered and incorporated in the worship design to make them comfortable and motivated to become a member of the fellowship. In terms of the method adopted by the church and/or the pastor used in the invitation to discipleship, it is extremely important that the preferences of the saved, unchurched, and the unsaved unchurched be communicated to the laity. This should help all involved to understand that method is everything and that the type of method could determine if an unchurched but saved person returns to the church, or if an unsaved person turns from the church. The method used could be the determining factor as to whether the sheep return to the fold and/or the lost sheep remain in the fold.

The Call to Discipleship

Church leaders must first communicate to the laity that some people are just not comfortable being led to the front of the church to become a member or to invite Christ into their lives. They must teach them that public confession can be done in various ways. Most of all, church leaders should communicate to their laity that if the plan of salvation is explained and prospective members understand and accept it then agree to be baptized, it matters not that it was done in the front of the church because the time of baptism is a public confession of one's faith and belief in Jesus Christ. When this message is conveyed to the laity, they would better understand when the pastor chooses to not bring an unchurched person under *scrutiny* where the audience becomes the inspector in the mind of the prospective member.

The Role of Laity in the Church

The role of laity in the church is vital to the survivorship of the church. When we have churches with leaders who have been properly discipled, we will have stronger more successful churches. Jesus made it abundantly clear that everyone should "deny themselves, pick up their cross, and follow Him." When we do as He has commanded, His blessings tend to follow. In starting up The Link Baptist Church, it was evident that people who had the same vision of caring for and loving on the loss were needed. When people with the common goal of desiring to share their "Jesus experience" with others, God does something supernaturally with their hearts.

The teachings of the life and love of Jesus is where we begin. Laity cannot teach others until they have been properly taught themselves. This takes time, and we must be patient with one another and wait on our Lord Jesus Christ to move on them as well as on us. When we come together to study and break down the Word of God, we believe that the Holy Spirit guides us in the direction that we should go. Learning the difference between self-effort and the work of the Holy Spirit is invaluable. Taking notes and using them later is one of the keys to success.

When Jesus is taught to laities, they must in turn, teach Jesus to others. The "Great Commission" is for all followers of Christ—not just church leaders. Likewise, when church leaders teach other church leaders, they must in turn, teach other church leaders, creating a good domino effect. When Jesus is the leader of any and all lessons, leaders and laity are changed; then and only then can they prayerfully teach others.

If church leaders are serious about building a true multicultural church, the laity must adapt to a lifestyle of specific spiritual standards and service. They must learn to live a disciplined life. They cannot afford to live any other way if they expect to project a good witness to the outside world and particularly in their church community. They must be transformed and live a Godly life. They must be vigilant and do the following:

1. Hold one another accountable. When we come together and ask each other the hard questions, God gets glorified.
2. Be dependable and mission-minded. Church leaders must accept the role of being "team Jesus" oriented.
3. Be responsible. Church members must acknowledge the fact that large and small tasks must be accomplished in the church. A perfect example is the restrooms must always be clean. Responsible leaders are willing to work wherever needed.
4. Be diligent. Do the work independently or assign others to do it. An observation is that people *do as you do* and sometimes *do as you say.*
5. Use various gifts and talents. Some of the strengths that laity possess as their chosen vocation can bring fresh insight and leadership to the church.
6. Assist the pastor. Help other church members to realize that the pastor is just one person who needs visionary leaders willing to come out of their comfort zones and help where they are needed. This includes strengthening the pastor with encouragement to continue in His God-given ministry. This is such a useful quality for all laity.
7. Be a good representative for the missional vision of the church. When the laity is strong in presenting the church mission and vision, it brings others into the fold, and when the new ones come in, they bring others into the fold. The lay people are living examples of true discipleship— committed to serving Jesus.
8. Have a sense of duty and obligation. When lay people feel that it is their duty to see that the work of the ministry must be fulfilled, the plans of God are extended to the congregation.

9. Be living examples. Some leaders work timelessly and unselfishly to ensure that God's plans are initiated and that the church is the growing body that God has called it to be.
10. Be fully committed to living out the Great Commission. The driving force behind the role of the laity is a *go* mentality.

> *And Jesus came and spoke to them saying, "All authority has been given to Me in heaven and on earth. Go therefore and make disciples of all the nations, baptizing them in the name of the Father and of the Son, and of the Holy Spirit, teaching them to observe all things that I have commanded you, and lo, I am with you always, even to the end of the age."* Matthew 28:18-20

We must seek inside and outside the church. Pastors and laity must have an intentional heart for seeking after the lost and truly making the case that everyone needs a savior—the only true Savior—Jesus Christ. When church leaders train laity to live the Christian life the way Christ intended, they become agents of change. They, in turn, become agents of change for others when they do likewise.

Goal Setting

Goal setting is one of the most important aspects of having a successful ministry. When congregants buy into the mission and vision of the church, the Lord will open the door for them to go outside and be true witnesses for our Lord, Jesus Christ. Church leaders and members must believe that they can be agents of change and make a difference in this world. They cannot give or accept excuses. Unity in goal setting and determination to fulfill the mission at hand must be our guide.

The Lord Jesus Christ calls us to be true moral agents of change.

When dealing with the lost and the unsaved, the Lord must give us His heart. We must not be ashamed to *love on* different people.

When believers accept the fact that God says we are all *one* blood, we can move forward and accept the challenges before us. How can we embrace anyone of a different culture if we cannot admit to some of the very same issues faced by the lost? All of us are so very different but possess some like qualities, and the Lord loves us all. No one should look down on others because they come from different cultures. The love of Jesus must be what compels us to make a difference by going out and sharing with people who do not look like us.

Chapter 3

THE LOST

More and more Americans are adopting their own values and disbanding those of their forefathers about the importance of attending church, resulting in a decayed society. Barna (2018) found that the reasons are varied among non-Christians and those who identify themselves as being Christian. Sixty-one percent of teens who profess to be Christians but do not view the church as being important stated that they find God away from the church. Approximately the same percentage (64%) of non-Christians say the same (Barna, 2018). The response of the non-Christians is easily understandable. However, the response of the Christian teens leads one to believe that perhaps their experience with church life has not been what it should have been; specifically, it has not been what God planned it to be. These statistics should cause the church to reexamine her purpose in serving those who profess to be Christians as well as those who do not. This is the reason *in-reach* is very important. While the church is called to do outreach, she is first called to teach, nourish and prepare those within the household of faith, as they will be the evangelists who will follow the mandate of our Lord and Savior, Jesus Christ, as penned by Luke: *"And the Lord said unto the servant, Go out into the highways and hedges, and compel them to come in, that my house may be filled"* (14:23). The children and teens are the church of today and tomorrow. Thus, the church must embrace and include them in a variety of activities that make them feel connected and teach them the importance of assembling, reminding them it is a dictate from the Holy Bible:

> *And let us consider one another in order to stir up love and good works, not forsaking the assembling of ourselves together, as is the manner of some, but exhorting one another, and so much the more as you see the Day approaching.* Hebrews 10:24-25

Evangelism is as important now as it ever was because without it, the Great Commission would fall down the tube. When church leaders pray together, permit God to lead and guide, teach and engage the children and youth, and serve the church community, they become more effective in their witness and increase their chances of fulfilling the command to do what is necessary to win souls for Christ, specifically people from varied cultures.

After a lengthy parable-based teaching on the nature of the Kingdom of God, Jesus asked His disciples:

> *"... Have you understood all these things?" They said to Him, "Yes, Lord." Then He said to them, "Therefore every scribe instructed concerning the kingdom of heaven is like a householder who brings out of his treasure things new and old."* Matthew 13:51-52

The teachings of Jesus on the Kingdom can and should serve as guiding principles for our own kingdom-building work. The church—God's product—should be the foundation on which order in modern day society rests.

Starting and growing new churches to advance the Kingdom of God is of the utmost importance. For the Word of God to be spread, there must be new avenues and approaches to reach the unsaved. Planting or starting new churches is Kingdom work, which is mostly basic in nature. Churches must be about fulfilling the purpose for its existence, which is wrapped up in the Great Commission: *"Go therefore and make disciples of all the nations..."* (Matthew 28:19-20). God commanded the church to evangelize to all; therefore, to do it effectively, the church must develop a plan.

The first underlying assumption in the church planting movement is to show the need for multicultural worship and its effectiveness. *Here's Life Crusade for Christ* found that people in multicultural communities are hungry for friendships and need someone to help them understand the new way. The organization also found that people in multicultural communities will be more relaxed or open to evangelism/ communication if they know they are loved. The second assumption is to make all who enter the doors of the church feel welcomed. Growth will only occur if the Lord and Savior, Jesus Christ, is the formula, the equation, and the answer.

The Joseph Generation

Exodus 1:8 states: *"Now there arose a king over Egypt, which knew not Joseph."* This scripture is referring to a generation of people who did not know the Lord. Within the past decade, a concentrated effort has been made to pull away from the church, causing the church to experience a drought. A huge number of people are simply not interested in attending any church, and conversations with pastors of different ethnicities, denominations, and creeds reveal a tremendous decrease in new believers attending church. Several factors that appear to be involved are listed below.

1. The rise in technology. The more sophisticated and knowledgeable society becomes about the world and life, the greater the resistance to know what God says or what God requires of us. Technology has taken the world to advanced heights of learning and sharing. It has proven to be a leading tool in the world, but not the best tool to

draw people to the church. It has many advantages, but one of the greatest disadvantages is that it has taken away time that should be dedicated to the Lord, as many have become addicted to using it, and others are distracted by it. The result is decreased fellowship in and with the church. The church uses modern technology to attempt to draw others, and oftentimes, it works. However, the questions: How much of it becomes about a *show* and How much becomes about *Jesus*? We are in the process of trying to find a good balance of how to use modern technology but not let it take over the intended purpose of the church and living for Jesus.

2. General Apathy. With so many man-made advances with tablets, phones, and artificial information, it seems as though people do not care about the things of God. There appears to be less affection for one another and more attention on oneself. When we, as a society, are more concerned about ourselves than our neighbors, we tend to be more introverted and self-centered. Self-centeredness has no place in kingdom-minded, kingdom-building churches. Not caring for one's neighbors, brothers, or sisters is an indication of a cold or hardened heart. This general feeling of non-caring apathetic emotions is isolating children in families, husbands and wives, believers and non-believers. What can we do to remedy this problem? How do we get people to care and share? How do we get people to come out of their comfort zones and love someone who is totally different? These are some of the issues that the church must be willing to confront, not later, but now.

3. Politics and Government. We live in an age of *nationalism* and not *globalism*. American and European countries appear to have a low tolerance for immigrants who are fleeing war-torn countries; however, the Lord has called the church and all believers to go above and beyond to reach

different people groups. The following conversation with the King places everything in perspective for all believers.

And the King will answer and say to them, 'Assuredly, I say to you, inasmuch as you did it to one of the least of these My brethren, you did it to Me.'

"Then He will also say to those on the left hand, 'Depart from Me, you cursed, into the everlasting fire prepared for the devil and his angels: for I was hungry and you gave Me no food; I was thirsty and you gave Me no drink; I was a stranger and you did not take Me in, naked and you did not clothe Me, sick and in prison and you did not visit Me.'

Then they also will answer Him, saying, 'Lord, when did we see You hungry or thirsty or a stranger or naked or sick or in prison, and did not minister to You?' Then He will answer them, saying, 'Assuredly, I say to you, inasmuch as you did not do it to one of the least of these, you did not do it to Me.' Matthew 25:40-45

We are to go a distance beyond the borders and be willing to love and share, help provide food, clothes, water, and Bibles; we are to meet needs. We must have a genuine love for humanity, regardless of what the government dictates. The political atmosphere is becoming more individualistic; the charge appears to be each nation must take care of itself and not cross borders to express and extend the true love of Jesus Christ. Has the political climate caused us to only see those near to us? What about those people who are far away and different? We, as believers, are under the kingdom authority of our Lord and Savior, Jesus Christ. When we obey the dictates of the spirit of the government and not the Holy

Spirit, the love of God is hindered. This new attitude of nationalism goes against the very fabric of who and what we are called to be.

Referencing the Bible, Israel's history includes generations that forgot about the Lord. This *not knowing Joseph Generation* is no different. We must embrace this generation with the same fervor and desire that our Lord expressed to us when He came after us. There are many in this *non-Joseph knowing generation* who are willing and ready to receive the message if we would only stand up and take it to them. We must have a heart for the lost and the unsaved to transform this generation into a generation that knows Joseph and for what he stood. When we take those values and standards into the world, we can, will and must make a generation that is ready to receive the love of Jesus Christ. We are commissioned moral agents of change. Let us get busy telling this world and generation about the challenges of Joseph, the love and overcoming, wonder-working power of Jesus.

Generation Z

Generation Z is the name assigned to individuals born between 1999 and 2015. Barna (2018) refers to this generation as being the first truly post-Christian generation, as they do not profess to have a religious identity. Barna (2018) found that the percentage of Generation Z teens that identifies as atheist is twice that of the adult atheists in in the United States; six percent of adults identify as atheist, while 13% of Generation Z identify as atheist. The study was conducted in 2016 and released in 2018. Six percent of the elderly, 5% of the Boomers, 7% of Generation X, 7% of the Millennials, and 13% of Generation Z identified as atheist.

A sizeable segment (37%) of Generation Z believes one cannot know for certain that God exists. Shockingly, 32% of adults in the United States believe likewise. The majority (54%) of the teens who believe an individual can know God do not profess they firmly believe it. Surprisingly, only 10% more adult believers (64%) do not profess they firmly believe an individual can know God exists (Barna, 2018).

Culture. Barna (2018) found that 58% of teenagers and 62% of adults believe Christianity is not the only true religion and that several religions can lead to eternal life. A significant number of teens, according to Barna (2018), believe that if one sincerely believes something, it is true. Like the Millennials, approximately half the teens note they need concrete evidence to confirm their beliefs. This is possibly why they are apprehensive on the topic of science versus the Bible.

Church attendance. While only a few attend church, Generation Z church attenders have a positive perspective of church as it relates directly to them. They find church to be the place where they learn how to have a meaningful existence. They also note that church is important to them (Barna, 2018). Approximately, 36%, however, feel that individuals who attend church are hypocrites. On the importance of attending church, only a few—5%—feel that attending church is very important. Twenty-seven percent feel church is not important at all (Barna, 2018).

What Must Be Done

The cultural and racial makeup of churches embracing multiculturalism must correspond with the church community or surrounding communities. More specifically, it must correspond to its target group. It gives members and guests from the multicultural community a feeling of representation. They see their own in positions of authority, resulting in less fear and a feeling that their interests will be recognized and appreciated more.

A lot of effort must be placed on building relationships. Methods to get people of different races and cultures within the congregation to become acquainted must be sought. Honest conversations between racial groups on the difficult and important topics of racism and cultural differences are necessary.

Challenges

Kidd and Howe reminded church leaders to anticipate problems. When the Lord instructed Pastor Bob and me to go out and start a new multicultural church, we had no idea as to the problems and obstacles that were before us. We reside in a city located in the heart or center of a southern state within the southeastern section of the United States. It has a long, dark history of institutional racism. The *god* of the city was money and separation. We knew that dealing with people would involve a conversation about one or the other. We dedicated several weeks and months in prayer before going out on our journey. God is good, and He is great, and we were determined to follow the Lordship of Jesus Christ. Below is a listing of some of the challenges we faced in establishing a multicultural church.

1. How to approach people who did not look like us. I am an American of African descent, and Pastor Bob is Anglo American. We both had to come out of our comfort zones and deal with racial issues on both ends of the spectrum. Jesus tells us about entertaining strangers unaware in Hebrews 13:1 and 2: *"Let brotherly love continue. Do not forget to entertain strangers, for by doing so some have unwittingly entertained angels."* We understood the message for us was to be ready to take time out to eat with someone new or different. Showing oneself friendly when meeting a stranger is the correct approach. It is needed in starting a simple conversation. Once people discovered that we were not selling anything or trying to get them to spend money, most were willing to converse with us about their salvation experience or to inform us as to if they knew Jesus. The scripture tells us to love our neighbor as ourselves Matthew 22:39: *"And the second is like it: You shall love your neighbor as yourself."* When we realize that most people will talk

or listen, we can overcome some of the obstacles that are before us as we witness for our Lord, Jesus Christ.

2. Apathy. One of the greatest challenges that we faced was apathy on behalf of believers and non-believers. It appeared we lived in a society where caring no longer existed. When other believers were asked to go out and share, oftentimes, it appeared that people were too busy. We know that the Lord has told us to go out and witness to the entire world. In His last commission, the Lord states: *"But you shall receive power when the Holy Spirit has come upon you; and you shall be witnesses to Me in Jerusalem, and in all Judea, and Samaria, and to the end of the earth"* (Acts 1:8). As I understood it, the Holy Spirit would empower and strengthen us to live and preach the gospel at every opportunity. We knew this meant we must first have a heart for God and His people. The believing Christians did not appear to have the heart to come out of their comfort zones and approach others. This feeling of apathy has grown to an even wider and deeper divide throughout the world. A great void surrounds the world because so many so-called believers and non-believers do not truly love Jesus. The love of Jesus is what propels the few believers who follow the great commission. How can we reverse this apathy? We must have an infectious enthusiasm that we pray will permeate the hearts and minds of other believers. It is so joyous when we see an unbeliever accept God's plan of salvation. To observe people who want and desire a change is very rewarding. When believers experience an unbeliever's salvation experience, it should challenge them to do more for our Lord Jesus; it is very rewarding to see people come to Jesus just as they are. This feeling of apathy will depart if more Christians invite other believers to go out into the public and witness for Jesus.

3. Fear of Rejection. When we are commissioned as believers to go out into the world, it is personal in our relationship

with Jesus. We must realize He was rejected by His own people (the Jews) and was somewhat rejected by the world. We, as believers, must realize we are not answering the great commission in our own strength, but in the strength of the Holy Spirit. God made us uniquely different. All ethnicities have different backgrounds and cultures; thus, Americans of African descent and Anglo Americans are no different. Do we not want to embrace others because they think we are judgmental? The different backgrounds and cultural experiences should be shared, understood, and embraced. The sharing, understanding, and embracing do not happen overnight; it takes time. We must embrace our differences and truly desire to learn about others and their culture. When we see that God has made us all the same, but different, we may be able to overcome the fear of rejection. We, in the church, must not allow fear to guide or control us. We must also remember, from a scriptural point of view, that our Lord, Jesus Christ, was rejected by His very own people and by many others: *"He came to His own, and His own did not receive Him"* (John 1:11); *"If the world hates you, you know that it hated Me before it hated you"* (John 15:18). Therefore, on our Christian journey, we will be rejected in many circumstances. We must not let fear, self-doubt, or rejection take us away from where God desires us to go.

4. Gotta have it right now mentality. Because of the advent and growth of technology, it is very difficult to deal with today's *gotta have it right now* generation. This generation tends to get bored quickly. They are more interested in social media and what is going on with their friends and peers. Social media has almost completely taken over this generation. Children are learning to use a phone, tablet or I-Pad before they learn the alphabets. Most worshippers between the ages of 20 and 30 are almost always faced downward, using mobile devices while attending worship

and praise service. Research results reveal this generation appears to be highly distracted by their mobile devices. It appears that at times, social media is the only thing in life worth dealing with. They want to like, share, and listen to others. The days of mailing letters are long gone, at least with this generation.

The super information highway has many advantages, but it also has many disadvantages. The rate at which social media is growing and attracting young minds is mind-boggling. They have access to other people in other countries at their fingertips. This *gotta have it right now* generation has not learned the fine art of patience and long suffering. Technology has taken learning, listening, gathering, sharing to a totally new and different level. Because this super information highway has taken over so many aspects of today's culture, it is difficult to reach the masses of young people. Church leaders must pray that the Lord will raise up a new generation of leaders who can take this technology and social media idea and learn from it. How can we get technology in the church and the church not lose the message of Jesus Christ? There are so many advertisements and distractions that come with the boom in technology. We must pray that the Lord raises up leaders who have a heart for His heart to reach the lost in this new generation and multicultural world.

We must, therefore, pray for Godly leadership to take us to this place where technology has taken society. If goodwill sends us leaders who can balance the truth of God's Word with the use of technology, we may be able to take the hearts and minds of this generation to a place where they see a need for a savior. Jesus is all; He is the only way: *"Jesus said to him, "I am the way, the truth, and the life. No one comes to the Father except through Me"* (John 14:6). We must pray that God will raise up leaders who are ready to influence this new generation of multicultural unbelievers. The world is influencing the church more than the church is influencing the world. Prayer is the answer and the key.

> *Lord Jesus, please help us to overcome these obstacles and find solutions to reach our children and grandchildren. Show us the way to reach other cultures and people groups for the Gospel of Jesus Christ. Amen*

If church leaders are serious about establishing a multicultural church, they will embrace these challenges and lead the church in not only establishing the new vision but in living it. They must be prepared to help those who do not believe diversity belongs in the church to understand God's command, as it is human nature to buy into something when the reason is clearly stated. People—church members in particular— must know why the church should be multicultural. Biblically, we are called to worship together. " *...Rejoice, O Gentiles, with His people!"* ... *"Praise the Lord, all you Gentiles! Laud Him, all you peoples!"* (Romans 15:10-11).

Kidd and Howe recommended selecting a multicultural team of leaders to pray for God's direction regarding His assigned people of other cultures to grow and serve within the fellowship. As aforementioned, prayer preceded everything in the establishment of The Link Baptist Church, and God's guidance was paramount. Kidd and Howe also noted that church leaders and laity should celebrate progress and evaluate, paying attention to how the congregants interact and communicate. They will need to learn how to identify warning signals such as lack of attendance and segregating into similar groups. Many congregants are so self-centered or engrossed in their own life circumstances, they do not think about checking on members who have been missing worship service or Bible study. Some believe that if God intended for cultures to blend, He would have blended them Himself. Church leaders will need to train the congregants in this area for the warning signs to be addressed. Most importantly, Kidd and Howe advise church leaders to lead in the communication efforts and to stay on top of problems to resolve them quickly.

Lewis and Wilkins assert that the church has the option of

choosing to confront reality or denying it. If the church is in denial while its goals of becoming multicultural are diminishing, its leaders may choose to do what is necessary to redesign its structure or continue in the direction they are going, which will lead to failure. What is needed is a spirit of unity among the multicultural leadership team members as they revisit the vision and direction God has for the church.

In their efforts to grow the church and reach across racial lines, one of the first things church leaders must do is create an atmosphere for worship that is appropriate for believers and unbelievers. Stetzer states: "The worship service should be God-centered or God-driven" (p. 268). Emphasis should be on the praise and worship experience and the Word, as God speaks through the sermon. Church leaders, however, must ensure the service is designed to meet the needs of unbelievers. In doing so, Stetzer notes that church leaders must not allow the needs of unbelievers to serve as a substitute, as the praise and worship experience should be Spirit-led, Christ-centered, and Bible-based.

How to Share the Gospel

First by trusting Jesus. Rock-solid faith is desperately needed of anyone considering evangelizing. We must remember that our God wants to work in us first, then through us to reach others for Him. One of the greatest gifts that the Lord Jesus gives to every believer is a heart to want to see others changed and saved. When we acquire a personal relationship with Jesus, we begin to understand what God requires of us. We then have a heart to simply walk out on faith and *just do it*. We understand that there are numerous barriers, distractions, and misunderstandings designed to plant fear in us to make us stand still. However, we must be constantly walking out the dictates of our faith. When we learn what God says in His Word, we must be willing to walk and work it out with others. James 2:14-17 states:

> *What does it profit, my brethren, if someone says he has faith but does not have works? Can faith save him?*

> *If a brother or sister is naked and destitute of daily food, and one of you says to them, "Depart in peace, be warmed and filled," but you do not give them the things which are needed for the body, what does it profit?*

> *Thus also faith by itself, if it does not have works, is dead.*

The scriptures speak proof that evangelism is *doing* the work of the ministry. We must be willing to go out and meet people where they are. Everyone needs the Gospel, the good news of Jesus Christ. Sharing Jesus and His love should be the primary goal of all believers. Church leaders or members trained in evangelism must be in expectation and receptive mode as God places non-Christians in their path, granting opportunities for association. Four effective principles of evangelism are listed below. Regardless of the method used, being sensitive is the key.

1. Vulnerability. Foremost in the evangelism process is a willingness to be vulnerable and open to others. Friendliness in an unfriendly and hostile world is necessary. Being opened to seeing people as Christ sees them is biblical: "And Jesus, when He came out, saw a great multitude and was moved with compassion for them, because they were like sheep not having a shepherd ..." (Mark 6:34). Meeting people by a simple introduction and ensuring them that you are not attempting to sell or market a product is fundamental. Doing so with a smile and a cordial personality opens doors to greet and earnestly learn how people are doing. Thus,

being friendly toward people, smiling, and listening are vital tools in trying to reach others for Jesus.

2. Listening and Speaking. Be willing to simply meet and converse with someone new and different. God created humanity with two ears and one mouth. His desire for us is to be careful hearers and speakers. Knowing when to listen and when to speak is key. People have concerns that we can pray about when sharing God's Word with them. Most people do not realize that the Lord has already addressed their concerns, troubles, trials, and tribulations in His Word. When we carefully listen, the Holy Spirit will lead and guide us on what to say next. We must be open to hearing God speak to us as believers in how to proceed in dealing with others in our witness of Him. The Lord encourages us in James 1:19: *"So then, my beloved brethren, let every man be swift to hear, slow to speak, slow to wrath."* We are encouraged to be careful and thoughtful listeners, to choose our words carefully, and be slow to become angry with others because of their sins, lifestyles, or decisions.

3. Personal Evangelism. Every Christian has a story. Telling others about the kindness and goodness of Jesus and how we were reeled in is relevant and is a good way to share. The adage *People don't care how much you know until they know how much you care* is real. Having a caring heart shows the world the love of God that compels us to do what we do. We must have a purpose and a mission to tell others how far we have come and from where the Lord has brought us. Assuring others of the kindness and goodness of Jesus, can be a motivator. It could prompt them to continue the conversation or engage in a deeper conversation.

Listening to people talk about their doubts and fears opens the door to discuss one's past unashamedly. We cannot be an effective witness if we exhibit a *super* Christian effect as if we have it together and have always had it together. When we tell others about how lost we were in our own personal sins, they oftentimes want to hear more. Personal evangelism at its finest is when Christians can tell others about their lostness and sins and how God delivered, changed, and transformed them. It is then and only then, that Christians can help free others from lostness: When we show others how the light and love of Jesus Christ drew us in, it makes a difference. Personal evangelism helps one to see others as God sees them. When we are made aware of the fact that we were once like them, we have a desire to want God to transform others as He transformed us. Personal evangelism is a mantra for all Christians.

4. Personal Prayer Life. When we purpose in our heart to spend time with the Lord in His Word every day, it transforms us. It also changes our perspective of others. The Lord left us with the powerful weapon of prayer. When we obtain a personal relationship with God, He shows us how to listen to Him in His Word in Christian songs and Godly teachings. Prayer is when we simply get down on our knees and talk openly and warmly with our Savior. God desires so much for us to talk with Him and to listen and be obedient when He speaks. Jesus states: *"If you love me, keep my commandments"* (John 14:15). He advises that everyone must pray. As Christians who want to see others saved, we must have a committed, connected, Christ-filled, and obedient prayer life. Prayer is the one difference maker that must never be excluded. It will give us the peace and answers that we need to proceed in effectively evangelizing the lost for Jesus.

These principles provide opportunities to learn about cultures and create an interest in the Gospel of Jesus Christ.

Stetzer states: "One of the most effective evangelistic methods a church can use is exposing the unchurched to the authentic worship of God. Unbelievers learn worship as they witness the worship of believers" (p. 269). Enthusiasm is what some believers are looking for in worship. Many want to experience what they see in authentic worship; they want to feel the enthusiasm or be a part of such an enthusiastic fellowship.

Since the church has been charged with serving the present age, it must move from oral to visual to secure and hold the attention of the worshippers--young people in general. Stetzer recommends the use of electronic communication through overheads, PowerPoint presentations, and video clips which enrich the worship experience. This would be a plus in a multicultural church where language may be a barrier to communication. The worshippers can visibly see the message that is being delivered if related graphics are projected on an overhead projector or projection screen.

To make a positive impact for our Lord Jesus Christ, we, the church, must be willing to accept the fact that we have not gotten it right. We must be willing to admit the error of our ways, and maybe then, the millennial generation and Generation Z will seek and listen to God's message. The following chapter consists of testimonials of adult members of the Link Baptist Church, 21 to 80 years of age. They are attempting to make a positive impact, providing words of encouragement and direction, while admitting mistakes so that the millennial generation and Generation Z will discover the identity crisis is not as alarming as it appears. The testimonials reflect various levels of spirituality, mentality, and emotionalism, pointing to Jesus Christ, the finisher of our faith (Hebrews 12:2). We pray that the reading of these personal authentic testimonies will positively impact the life of the reader specifically, and this world in general. What a wonderful and beautiful name it is--the blessed name of Jesus!

Thank you so much, Jesus, for your love, goodness, and kindness. Thank you, Jesus.

Testimonials

Barriers and Opportunities to Linking the Lost to the Lord
Personal Testimony as a Praise and Worship Leader
Adrianna Cooper-Jones

Psalm 145, a Davidic hymn, states: *"I will extol You, my God, O King; And I will bless Your name forever and ever."* This prayer of worship, praise, and adoration is the score to the opus of my life. I mean it when I sing, *I love you, forever, I praise you forever, Lord!* He is that to me—God, King, Lord. He has purchased my salvation with His precious blood, and I will praise Him all the days of my life for His goodness, for His safety, for His blessings, for His faithfulness to a poor wretch like me--the seventh child of 15--the next to the baby girl who was supposed to be another statistic. In 1990, shortly after the death of my eldest brother, the song titled *Thank You, Lord* was written by Edwin Hawkins, acclaimed worship leader and man of God.

> *Tragedies are common; all kinds of diseases are prevalent, people are slipping away, economies are up and down, incomes are low for the majority of people, but as for me, all I can say is "Thank you Lord, for all You have done for me!"*

I can say this because He delivered me from abject poverty, provided me with a world-class education to which I could not have afforded, and positioned me to take care of my mother in her old age, raise her youngest child after her death, and purchase my first home! He has been my battle ax in the time of battle, my shield, and my buckler. When the enemy came in like a flood ... He was the standard (Isaiah 59:19). The psalmist, Fredrick Whitfield wrote: *Oh, how I love Jesus, "Oh, how I love Jesus, Oh, how I love Jesus, because HE first loved me*!

Knowing but Not Doing

We are fortunate to be living in a time where education and experiences have provided us with so much knowledge of what we should do. However, we fail at execution. The world calls it "*failure to launch*." They know what to do, how to do it, and when it should be done. They can converse easily and effortlessly with us about what they should do. However, the reality of life is that their conversation, text messages, and social media footprint do not add up to results. In evaluating the actions of these individuals, it is often discovered that there is no evidence to support what they say they believe, know, and understand--especially regarding their faith.

The Legacy Lost: The Need for a Link

How exactly did we lose are connection to our faith in the Lord? Why do we need to be linked back to Him? Generation X dropped the ball and Generation Y changed all the rules of play. We are upwardly mobile as a right we take for granted, which was really a gift, a gift from the generations of our ancestors who endured the hardships of racial discrimination, religious persecution, and gender bias. They marched when they could have accepted the status quo; they walked when they could have chosen to ride, and they stood up when they could have sat down to provide us with access, opportunity, and mobility. We received these precious gifts and forgot the source from which all good and perfect gifts are bestowed.

The Lost

Consequently, my generation--those in their late 30s and early 40s--can achieve so much in the way of material things, without directly inquiring of the Lord, Jesus. We earn degrees and credentials, purchase cars and homes, develop relationships that produce children, and when life goes awry as it often does, we can secure solutions. For example, when we need to finance schooling, we go to financial aid; when we need a car, we can use co-signers or avail ourselves to *buy here pay here* car lots, and when we fail to receive something from our spouse that we feel we need, we can always get a divorce. There is very little we feel we need from God or his darling Son--Jesus, until we are faced with the tragedies of life. Therefore, we save Jesus as our final resort. We save Him for what we cannot fix ourselves with our own wit, savvy, swagger, or money. The trials of life provoke us to seek out the Almighty God. The Love Fellowship Choir sang about these trials: *Folks without homes, living out in the streets/And the drug habits some say, they just can't beat/Muggers and robbers, no place seems to be safe.* I believe the songwriter is testifying to what has been my personal experience with the Lord. However, to properly introduce the lost and unsaved to our Lord, we must accept that they are where they are and be willing to reach them through contemporary, relevant praise and worship, and dynamic discipleship and training.

In the beginning of our journey, most of us only began to attend church regularly when we began having children. This is because our parents took us to church. However, our lives did not merit change until the adversities of life could not be met by our intellect, street savviness, or our personal situations became so dire they demanded the miraculous actions of God. It is in these times that we seek Him, yield to Him, and rely upon Him. Sadly, we succumb to all forms of adversity and agony due to our poor life choices. It is only when we become down trodden and are about to be overwhelmed by all that is wrong with our lives that we are in the perfect place for God to transform our hearts to become receptive to developing a true relationship with the Lord.

Many of the lost only seek the Lord out of a need for a solution to their situation: illness, incarceration, and/or financial insecurity. This sets the stage for failure in most cases. When our motives are not pure, when we go to the Lord out of habit, or seek a handout, we create the climate for those who come in on fire, often wane after a few months, and become backslidden or lost to the seduction of the world.

Hope

I declare that the stronghold can be broken from your heart and mind. You do not have to continue to be a victim of your brokenness! You can release "forever" in exchange for "never." Instead of bombarding Heaven with your anger, hurt, and envy ... consider this: What if your hope for a forever had been a never? What if your body does not become sick, and you never get on your knees to meet Jesus as a healer? What if the mother you are given chooses the option to not keep you? ... or what if you have been horribly abused or neglected by the people who should provide and protect you? I cannot change those facts, but I know from personal experience that you can be healed and made whole despite these type situations.

What if my brothers do not die as young men and my marriage does not fail? Let us be transparent. If my heart never gets broken, and I hold on to the idea of *forever*, would I be on this part of my faith journey? Would I be willing and able to *"declare the works of the Lord in the land of the living"*? (Psalm 118:17) I can say firmly that if none of these trials of life had not occurred, my faith would never be matured, my dreams would never have been realized, and my God would not be glorified in this very moment! I am so grateful for my journey that I refuse to belittle my pain or discount my shame. I will not deny His glory by not telling my story. I will not cry about a lost *forever* when the alternative to my pain and your pain is to *never*—to never have experienced God's love, mercy and grace. As a result, I can identify the barriers the church faces in linking this generation back with the Lord, but I also see amazing opportunities.

Opportunities

Proper discipleship is vital to the transformation from unsaved to saved; the reborn must be re-educated in the ways of God. We do not know the ways of God, and we only know for certain what we have lived within our human experience. Hence, discipleship of the babe in Christ is vital to conversion, deliverance, and servanthood. The recipe for reaching them is teaching them discipline and the significance of service to the Lord and His people.

Matthew 7:7 declares: *"Ask, and it will be given to you; seek, and you will find; knock, and it will be opened to you."* The process by which one is disciplined is a process of seeking correction, finding out the truth, and submitting to God's way, and not our own. It is an exercise in humility and constant failure. On this journey, we must humble ourselves to accept redirection and accept that we may fail more than we succeed, but we must be committed to the process of transformation. Turning our ways over to His ways requires that our dealings with people, places, and things be altered and aligned with the Word of God, that we might be "washed by it" so that we can be transformed into Christ-likeness.

The Lord requires us to do something about what we believe. The doing looks like this: You take your gifts and talents, time, and abilities to bless the kingdom of God, especially His people and those that are in the greatest need. Isaiah 1:17 states: *"Learn to do good; Seek justice, Rebuke the oppressor; Defend the fatherless,*

Plead for the widow." My big brother says it like this, "We have to invest ourselves, our time, and our abilities into being a blessing for the Lord." That means you must give the gift He has given to you to others. Ultimately, while you are doing something about what you believe, the Lord can perform a miraculous blessing inside of you that will transform you. If we teach new converts how to do this by serving in their local church, their, community, and their state, they will honor God with the work of their hands and the fruit of their lips, and in the process, their hearts will be transformed by the Lord. They will turn to God and Jesus, His Son, for a relationship with Him instead of results from Him.

The POP Method of Teaching
Angelia Denson

As a Sunday school teacher, I find that one can obtain better results when using a proven method of teaching. While there is no *one* guaranteed method, choosing one that has produced good results should be acceptable. Knowing how to get started proves to be the toughest first step. It could prove to be a great tool for discipleship when instructing others on preparing lessons or studies, as teaching others should be a direct byproduct of having been taught.

The first "P" in this method is *Preparation.* Preparation has to do with the process of making oneself ready to do something. In this situation, it is to teach. Being filled with the Holy Spirit through prayer and communion with the Lord is essential before anything else can flow. One must prepare himself or herself spiritually before trying to do anything. Invoking God's anointing, presence, and power will produce what is needed to research, read, and record notes.

Possessing materials that enhance one's studies is vitally important. Teachers should possess a wealth of research and study materials and use them to supplement their lessons. One valuable tool used at The Link Baptist Church is the *Thompson Chain Reference Study Bible.* Using this study Bible requires time and dedication. However, it is well worth it; its reference verses, character studies, and numerical index takes the process to another level.

After spending time in prayer and acquiring appropriate study material, one must be willing to sacrifice time and dedication to studying. A teacher should be familiar with his or her notes and material to the point where the notes simply serve as a guideline. Reading the first couple of words automatically refreshes the mind, as the presenter will have organized and planned well.

The *O* stands for *Operation.* Operation involves the performance or function of actions that produce results. To obtain results, something must be done to bring about an outcome. Delivering research results and studies in a way that the class grows and matures should be the sole desire of every teacher. Not having the listening audience glean from the teaching-learning process proves useless. Isaiah 55:11 states:

So shall My word be that goes forth from My mouth;

It shall not return to Me void,

But it shall accomplish what I please,

And it shall prosper in the thing for which I sent it.

When we do our part in preparing to learn and properly present God's Word, it will serve His intended purpose.

Being on the receiving end of a well-taught lesson should make the students appreciate the effort and time dedicated by the teacher. When teachers operate in their calling, the class benefits, and the Lord is glorified. However, when this is not the case, both the class and the teacher suffer, and the Lord is not glorified. When more faith and trust is put in the Word of God and the Holy Spirit than in self-effort, Philippians 4:13 becomes a reality: *"I can do all things through Christ who strengthens me."*

The final *P* stands for *Participation*. Participation involves action—taking part in something. An endeavor or task cannot be successful unless someone takes an active part in completing it. Without participation, nothing happens. To be successful at teaching, student engagement is the key; there must be active participation. Teachers at The Link Baptist Church entertain open dialogue with their disciples, getting them involved in the teaching-learning-process. Providing opportunities to ask questions and give input allow teaching and learning to become more personal. Each lesson should make the disciple ask: "How does it relate to me?" The responses and questions of others enable disciples to understand that their questions are not dumb or stupid and that most likely someone else had the same thought. Active participation on the part of disciples also assists the teacher in determining level of understanding of what is being taught; instead of assuming, the teacher knows.

Asking the right questions that make individuals think deeply sparks responses that add to the depth of the lesson. It has been my experience on many occasions that responses or questions from the disciples have caused me to think deeply. Everyone learns and grows from active participation and hearing what the Holy Spirit has said to others. A vibrant and thriving Sunday School is the result of inclusion, involvement, and embracement. Everyone should feel like they have a voice if their comments pertain to the subject at hand. Knowing when and how to reel the dialogue back in and on the topic without intentionally offending anyone is crucial.

Putting into *practice preparation, operation,* and *participation* has been rewarding to me as a teacher. I believe adhering to this method will bring positive results to those who actively use it. Although there is not a sure-proof method when dealing with people, the one absolute is the Holy Spirit. He will always lead and guide in the right direction, never failing. Regardless of what people want to do or hear, He knows what is best.

The Lord, The Link, The Lost
Pastor Kenneth McMillan
Loving Kindness and Everlasting Love

Parents have entertained this generation of children. The children and teenagers have the same expectations as the parents. They believe that there should be an entertainment component to the church. In Jeremiah 31:3, he tells the people what God said to him:" *Yes, I have loved you with an everlasting love; therefore, with loving kindness I have drawn you."* The modern-day family must learn that the biblical definition of "loving kindness" is the love of God, and the kindness of God. The love of God should be enough to sustain any and everyone. In Jeremiah 31:3, the people of God were severely under attack, so God made a way of assuring them that His Holy and divine favor would sustain them in their time of need, and it was done with His *everlasting* love. This was a covenant that God made throughout scripture. It started with Abraham in Genesis 15: 7-21 and with another covenant God made with the nations of Israel (those who represent the people of God in Exodus 19:3-8 and Deut. 28: 1-30:10). This is very important because God has always promised to be our faithful God if we would be His faithful people. God has vowed throughout the Bible to be faithful to us if we remain faithful to Him. Faithfulness is akin to loyalty. If we remain humble, faithful, and loyal to God, He will be faithful to us. He will shower us with blessings, protect, and provide for us. He has vowed to remain faithful to all commitments. Israel and the people of God can look forward to a future of hope in expecting and experiencing the sweet promise and blessing that God has in store for His people who are patient, loyal, and faithful.

Entitlement

Because we, the members of the Link Baptist Church, possess a strong desire and a personal sense of urgency to reach this generation, we are asking God to give us His eyes to see what He is seeing and His ears to hear what He is Hearing. In gathering to discuss observations of problems within the family, I experienced a lack of support from the men in helping to solve the problem of how to effect change and appeal to this generation. In attempting to listen to the voices of our young people and parents, we wanted God to put us in receptive mode so we could hear what HE was hearing. My personal view was that so many young people and parents today have this feeling of *entitlement*. They seem to think that if they show up at church, they should be rewarded. It appears to be a pattern of expectation held by the younger generation. Is this a learned behavior stemming from children being bribed into doing some reasonable service or chore at home? The attitude of entitlement at home has spilled over into the church. Some parents are bringing non-biblical ways of parenting into the church and expecting the church to conform to their ways. The church can never compromise its value system to please some children and families who have a sense that they are entitled to negotiate with God's ways and His Word. The entitlements are learned attitudes and behaviors that are often accepted at home. Some parents have become more friends than parents to their children. The family should be redirected to follow and obey God and His Word first, and not allow the children to run the family. I have witnessed where some children will tell their parents what they will and will not eat. If the parents do not stand up for righteousness and to the Word of God, who will do it?

The people of God, and the church must be willing to take a loving well-balanced stand for the Word of God. God has given the power and authority to the parents to be the decision makers in the home. Proverbs 22:6 states: *"Train up a child in the way he should go: and when he is old, he will not depart from it."* Again, we have proof and evidence of God's expectation. The word *train* denotes that God gives authority to do something. Parents are called to challenge their children to be all they can be. They should encourage their children to become well educated and to make a difference in the world and not to have an expectation that somebody is going to give them something simply because they show up.

Hope Does Not Disappoint
Geraldine McMillan

If we allow ourselves to be engrossed in the ugliness, darkness, murdering, and destruction in the world, we will become numb, unloving, unforgiving, vengeful, helpless and hopeless. To progress through our earthly journey, we must seek first the face of Jesus, the Kingdom of God (Matthew 6: 33), look for the beauty in His creation, and accept the love which He has for each of us. It is true that we will experience storms, trials, pain, disappointments and tribulations, but I believe wholeheartedly that Jesus is in total control. He will never leave nor forsake us, but we must *believe*, have *faith*, and keep *hope* alive. I am thankful and grateful that in our darkest hour, we can always read and *meditate* on Romans 5:1-5:

> *Therefore, having been justified by faith, we have peace with God through our Lord Jesus Christ, through whom also we have access by faith into this in which we stand, and rejoice in hope of the glory of God. And not only that, but we also glory in tribulations, knowing that tribulation produces perseverance; and perseverance, character; and character, HOPE. NOW (at this very moment) HOPE does not disappoint, because the Love of God has been poured out in our hearts by the Holy Spirit who was given to us.*

God's Word is the blueprint for life. In it, we find faith, hope, and charity.

*Thank you, Jesus ✝

Walking the Talk
Twila Gitschlag

To reach this generation for Christ, we must have something that others want. I know we are supposed to have what others want, but if we are not living what we say we believe, then do we really have something that they want? We cannot be like the world or the status quo.

1 Peter 3:15 states: *"But sanctify the Lord God in your hearts, and always be ready to give a defense to everyone who asks you a reason for the hope that is in you, with meekness and fear."* If people are not asking you about the hope that is within you, then you are either not showing the hope or you are not hanging around those who need your hope. If most Christians are just striving to get by or perhaps know a few scriptures but are not *walking* what they say they believe, then there is no love and no attraction.

The question: How do we reach the next generation for Christ? is a question that each generation has asked. Yes, it might be harder than ever, but according to the Bible, during the end times, even the elect will fall away. So why are we surprised that this generation wants nothing to do with the little church or the big church? That does not mean we should not strive to reach them. There was a Vacation Bible School song several years ago about letting our actions match our passions. If we are truly passionate about Christ, that passion will come through our actions—how we live.

If we truly love God with all our heart, soul, mind, and strength, we will see the needs of others and strive to meet those needs and truly love others. It is Christ's love in us that will attract all generations to Him. The problem is that there is a disconnect between what we say we believe and how we act. We will not be able to reach others for Christ until that disconnect is fixed and we truly fall in love with Christ.

Prayer
Pamela Paul

Prayer is an act of communication with God. Many believe they need other people to pray for them as though they are not capable of talking to God on their own, or because they are unable to speak eloquently. We often think that prayer depends on us, but it does not. It does not depend on our performance, but it depends on our relationship with Jesus Christ. It is good to know when we pray, we are not alone; Jesus is with us, and as we ask in His name, He relays our prayers to God, the Father. Despite our heartfelt prayers, things do not always go the way we desire, but we must keep the faith and not lose heart. We need to understand that we do not always need to ask for something when we pray. At times, we need to send up prayers of thanksgiving. We also need to be aware that the answer may not always be *yes*. Sometimes, it is *wait*. At other times, it may be *no*. This is where one's faith comes into play. What does one do? He or she must wait patiently on the Lord without trying to fix the situation, because oftentimes, trying to fix *it* causes bigger issues.

If you have ever struggled in your prayer life, know that you are not alone. We all have struggled. Some have struggled to the point of turning away from the Lord. Many problems and troubles drive us to pray, but often, our pride blinds us to how needy we really are and makes us rely on ourselves, rather than on God. Knowing that we have great need for prayer, why is it often the last resort? The answer is *selfish pride*. We have been given an all-inclusive model for prayer recorded in the Gospel of Matthew (6:9-13). It is good for any situation and is always fitting.

In this manner, therefore, pray:
Our Father in heaven,
Hallowed be Your name.
Your kingdom come.
Your will be done
On earth as it is in heaven.

Give us this day our daily bread.
And forgive us our debts,
As we forgive our debtors.
And do not lead us into temptation,
But deliver us from the evil one.
For Yours is the kingdom and the power and the glory forever.
Amen.

Praise Dance: My Safe Haven
Keshea Paul

Have you ever been in a rough point of your life, where you wish you could escape from everything and everyone? I have been there, and my only and best escape was my worship. I always had a passion for dance, but not necessarily glorifying God through dance. It was not until my life, as I knew it, began to crumble around me, that I learned to love God more than my problems. It was hard to press through the pain; however, pressing on was necessary. When I understood that, praise dance became my escape from the world of hurt. I could turn on some music and allow myself to escape to a place where it was only God and myself. It was an intimate haven. In that haven, the wounds of physical abuse began to heal, the weight of my failing marriage began to be lifted, and the thought of suicide began to fade away; the weight of hurt and pain was not mine to bear alone. Praise dance was a way to release everything to God—the one who could help me move forward.

I do not want to mislead anyone to think praise dance will fix all problems, because it will not. Only Jesus Christ can do that. Learning more about the Word of God and applying it to my life has changed me—from living a promiscuous life to seeking holiness—from seeking love in all the wrong places to finding unconditional love. When the Word of God changed me, I started making better choices, and my circumstances began to change for the better. I must admit a lot of what I went through was because of my bad choices, but through Jesus Christ, I am totally forgiven and loved. Understanding this has truly blessed me.

That Special Day
Octavious Smith

After only a short time at The Link Baptist church, I felt loved because two of the people I loved, respected, and trusted were already members—Mr. and Mrs. Agee. They had already shared many things about me with other members, so after going a few times and being welcomed with opened arms, I knew it was where I wanted and needed to be. I just could not say that I was ready to join; however, once I did, I knew it was the Lord leading me to do so. I will never forget the moment I talked to Pastor Ken and told him I wanted to be baptized. I shared my dream with him— Minister Agee was in the pulpit preaching the day of my Baptism. Pastor Ken said, "Do you know what?" I responded, "What?" He said Minister Agee would be the one preaching next Sunday. I smiled with amazement! The same day, Pastor Ken called a few members back into the church, and I publicly announced that I wanted to be baptized. At that moment and time, it was much better than the dream. It was so amazing, because not only was Minister Agee preaching that day, he and Minister Paul were also in the baptismal pool with me, with the assistance of a few other ministers and/or deacons.

The day everything happened was the day I discovered the true meaning of baptism. Going in the water and being resurrected was a moment I never will forget. I remember on the way back to change into my baptismal clothing, my favorite song was playing: *Cooling Water*, by the William Brothers. I felt something that felt like chills, but I knew it was God's Spirit all over me. I will never forget that day and that feeling. Going in and out of the water felt so surreal, but every time I think about that special day, the more real it becomes. Being baptized has brought me even closer to Jesus Christ. It was an unbelievable feeling. Although, I knew the Lord before my experience, this move gave me something I never thought was important—a church home. I also found a family I love who loves me, also.

The Journey Called Life
Michelle Harper

On this journey called life, God has really shown Himself faithful and true. I have made many bad decisions—some of which should have cost my life. However, they left me disconnected from God. I refused to harken to the voice of the Lord and ended up becoming disobedient, angry, bitter, unforgiving, and unloving. Growing up in the church as a little girl, I really did not understand what church was about, but I loved how the music and the sound of the older mothers singing made me feel. As I grew older and became an adult, God was still there, always talking and directing me. However, I still was not willing to surrender because I still wanted to do what I wanted to do. By not living the life God planned for me, I failed myself, friends, people who saw me as a role model, my parents, grandparents, and most of all, God. I can only blame myself. I chose the life I desired, and I have lived with regrets and pain. However, through it all, He— GOD—never left my side, and for that I am grateful. Psalm 139:8b states: *"If I make my bed in hell, behold, You are there."*

Doing things my way, trying to be someone that I was never designed to be, has made an adverse impact on my three daughters. I see in them what I saw in myself, a lack of confidence and low self-esteem and it stems from one person—me. I was selfish and unwilling to listen. I have now turned everything and everyone over to God. Initially, He was nowhere in the equation or the solution. In Sunday school, we talk about what kind of legacy we will leave behind. Three to four months ago, my response would have been a sure ticket to HELL, but now, I am in a better/right place with God. I want people to know that their life is not their own. If I had allowed God to be the head of my life, leading and guiding me from the beginning, I would not have gone down that dark road.

Many women come to the unfortunate conclusion, after becoming parents, that it is very difficult to raise sons and daughters in the home with their fathers who are present only in body. They overcompensate by attempting to be both mother and father—not truly understanding the damage it causes. They seek to raise their children in a positive environment at least like the one in which they were reared. However, sadly they find that overcompensating is not the solution.

I was reared without my father, but my father and grandmother always spent time with my sister and me. As time passed and my girls became young ladies, we were faced with bigger problems. I grew angry and again permitted hatred to enter in my heart as I reminisced about my mother and father not being together. To compensate for what I feared my children were experiencing, I attempted to resolve the issue by buying them material things. I was so confused that I gave them too much, trying to fill the void.

I used my children as my excuse for dealing with bitterness. I can admit now that I did not handle the situation in a Godly way, nor did I pray and ask God to lead and guide me. I realize that the more I gave to my girls, the more I was creating a bigger demon inside of them. At one point, my oldest daughter *tried* me. I corrected her quickly, letting her know that I was still her mother. I realized I was acting more like my children's friend. It is okay to have fun with your children, but always let them know you are the parent, not their friend or their equal.

Life experiences taught me that since I did not have a mother-daughter relationship with my mother, I found myself doing, acting, and saying some of the same things I had experienced with my mother. Where does it end? I decided to allow God's Word to truly minister and speak to me. I needed some blocks to be broken in my life. I refused to walk around another year holding on to pure hatred in my heart for the woman who was God's choice to be my mother. What role did I play in this situation? I did not want to admit that I was as guilty or guiltier than my mother. We are so quick to accuse or point fingers at the other person, but what do we do to attempt to solve the problem? I saw her mistakes and failures, but I refused to see mine. Jeremiah 29:11 states: *"For I know the thoughts that I think toward you, says the Lord, thoughts of peace and not of evil, to give you a future and a hope."* To obtain His plans for my life, I had to be broken first—all the way to the ground. I had to admit and surrender to His will and His way. Life is like a roller coaster; one day you may be up and happy, and the next day you may be down and sad. However, through it all, we must continue to press and never give up. My goal is to live a life that is pleasing to God—not man. Stay encouraged and Love like God told us to love—*unconditionally. God bless you all.*

My Faith Journey
Bennie (Karmin) Baker

*"Now faith Is the substance of things hoped for and
the evidence of things not seen."* Hebrews 11:1

Please take a short walk with me on my faith journey. Ready, set—here we go! As a young man born in the 60s, my father lost his battle with cancer when I was only 11 years old. Along with my brothers and sisters, I was raised in a home by a mother who trusted and believed wholeheartedly in the Lord. She loved her family deeply and ruled with a firm hand. I longed for the day that I would finish school, leave home, and venture out to see the world! In the meantime, I would continue to hang out on the street corners day after day, drinking and indulging in mischief with my homies—my road dogs. My eyes would soon be opened to the *goodness, grace* and *mercy* of God. Fast forward:

Phase 1: The year is now 1998, and I am attending a wrestling event. Normally, it is a family affair; oddly, I attend alone. Midway through the event, I take a restroom break. Moments later, I wake up on the floor. I glance upward as the steady flow of spectators walk aimlessly past me. No one asks if I am alright, nor do they offer to help. Are they assuming that I am just another man who had too much to drink? Perhaps that is what they were thinking, but that was not the case—not on this night. I was 100 percent sober. I gather my composure, adjust my cap, and return to the event to continue watching until the end. I take another bathroom break before driving home, and again, I lose consciousness in the restroom. I awaken—for the second time—pull myself up and make the drive home. I bypass the hospital—just yards away—where I clearly need to be. By the *true grace* of God, I get home without hurting anyone or myself. I wake my wife to tell her that I think my heart is beating too fast. She peers up at my face. I am soaked with sweat pouring down my face. There is no need to check my heart rate because my body is rocking, and my heart is pounding with such force and speed that she cannot count the beats. We make the drive to the Emergency Room where I am seen immediately. The EKG reveals I am having a Supraventricular tachycardia (SVT), which is an abnormally fast heart rhythm that comes from improper electrical activity in the upper part of the heart: At this point, my heart rate is in excess of 225 beats per minute. I am given medications to slow it down, which bottoms out my blood pressure. "Lord, please help me Jesus!" They lower my head downward and raise my feet up. Eventually, my heart starts to slow down, but the rhythm is off. In the days to follow, the cardiologist performs a heart catheterization, orders more tests, and prescribes an array of medications. It is determined that my heart problems are caused by a heart defect known as an atrial septal defect—a hole between the left and right ventricles of the heart.

Phase 2: Open heart Surgery to repair the defect.

Phase 3: Fluid has built up around my heart. I am now facing my second open heart surgery two weeks later; yet, God continues to bless.

Phase 4: The heart muscle has become weakened, and I am made aware of my options because it is pumping at about 10 percent with a heart transplant being one option. I am sent to an electrophysiologist who determined I would benefit from an AICD, an implantable Defibrillator. Another surgery? One diagnosis after another—SVT, atrial fibrillation, congestive heart failure! After my initial defibrillator, it was discovered that there was a recall on one of the leads that was inserted into my heart. I would undergo several more surgeries, including a generator changeout—a battery change. The one changeout that truly tested my faith was when a different physician improperly implanted the replacement. The device literally worked its way out of my chest, causing a massive infection, which could have claimed my life—but GOD! I underwent another surgery to remove the device; it was quite visible. I looked down at my chest and I, my original electrophysiologist, the PA, and my wife, were all horrified. I had looked at it for two weeks. Was that a foolish move—not seeking treatment? In retrospect, of course it was! —but GOD! The device and infected surrounding tissue had to be removed. My chest wound would require a plastic surgeon. The scar that would remain resembling the letter *J*, I would later say it stands for *Jesus*, and this scar would serve as a constant reminder of how close man thought I was to death—but GOD!

I was in ICU for a few days because I could not get a new device until they were certain the infection was gone. I looked back over all my scars and reflected over those last years, and I was sure that beyond a shadow of a doubt Jesus heard me, and I heard Him. I lay there for days without that device in my chest which was designed to control every beat, and to fire, more like a *mule kicked* me in the chest if the rhythm became life threatening. It dawned on me that Jesus is my rhythm and that my faith is not in the wisdom of men, but in the power of the almighty God (1 Corinthians 2:5). I thank Him for the affliction. I do not know where I would be if He had not saved my life and my soul. I know it is Jesus Christ, my Lord and Savior, who kept me safe, and I know it is God and God who will keep me throughout my life. By His stripes, I am healed!

Stand for Christ
Clemetine (Ron) Agee

My husband and I are in our late 60s. We met in college, married and within a few months, had our first child—a son. My husband was raised in the inner city of Detroit by a single mom. His dad was killed when he was approximately 12. I was raised in a rural town in north Alabama, first by a single mom who lived with her grandparents until she married; I was approximately four years old. Our backgrounds were very different and immediately began to show up as the two of us began our family, being only 20 years old.

While residing in Detroit, we were confronted almost daily with drugs, alcohol etc., but my husband's grandmother was a presence and force for Christ. Working in a factory to support a wife and a baby was difficult, and the street life was a constant threat. Suddenly, that threat was no longer present, as Uncle Sam called, and he was drafted into the Army. I went back to my family in Alabama with our infant son. We lived with my mom and dad and resumed my life in the church and community where I was reared. I was connected, but my husband was still disconnected, especially from a growing son. We were also disconnected as husband and wife. Trouble was present, and seeing how vulnerable we were, we arranged to reunite when he was stationed in Ft. Benning Georgia.

We were separated again when my husband was stationed in Alaska, and my son and I remained in Columbus, Georgia. Life spiraled out of control as we "did our own thing" in separate places. I was going to church but not really living the life until a friend introduced me to her church, where her father was pastor. I began a spiritual journey that changed my life, but my husband was a long way from us and God. We managed, however, to stay married until the army discharged him, at which time we reunited. It was difficult for the three of us to live together after the long separation. Our son was approximately eight years old at that time and resented his father coming back and taking over as *man of the house*. Their relationship remained strained, as my husband was a strict disciplinarian. Marital problems began, and parenting issues mounted as we moved from a *single mom* type of household to a two-parent household. We were saved, but our lives still reflected too much of us and not enough of Christ.

We had a second child. We say she grew up after Christ—AC— not witnessing the mess that we were. We had, with the help of the Lord, defeated some demons. We kept the rest hidden from our daughter. However, we could not hide it from our son. We became *sold out* for church and were almost constantly at the church for choir rehearsals, meetings, church service, etc. We were so involved that we had very little family time or time for school activities. We thought that was what God required for us to be good church members. The question is: "Did we lose the children?" It appeared we were at church more than we were at home. However, we appeared oblivious to the many negative influences that were impacting families like ours, e.g. gangs in schools, teenage pregnancies, alcohol and drugs etc. Should we have taken more family time and incorporated God in those times?

Fast forwarding, we eventually were set free and began to have a Christian *walk* that more closely resembled our Christian *talk*. Both our children are grown, and we are proud of their accomplishments. We are especially grateful that they are caring adults. We will never stop praying and believing for both to have and maintain a close relationship with Jesus Christ.

My son has two sons. My daughter has two daughters. For years, they loaned us these very different grandchildren, and we had a chance to do with them what we perhaps did not do with our children. They spent every weekend with us, and we had Sunday school with them on Saturday night and took them to church on Sunday and to Bible study on Wednesdays. We attended their sports events, took them on trips, and had a good time with them while attempting to instill the values of Christ. They are very different, and to a large degree, have formed their own views of life. It is obvious to us that each of these generations is dealing with life, God and faith in Christ very differently. Yet, each generation influences the next. The challenge for us is to stand for Christ and His ways in this present age. We are sometimes at a loss because we are largely out of touch with them and their technological existence. The eldest has graduated college and is teaching. His brother is in college. One is a senior in high school, and her sister is in a charter school. What does their world consist of? Their world consists of reliance on social media and the super information highway, communicating less traditionally and more via technology.

More importantly, how do we keep ourselves and our Lord Jesus relevant in their lives? We seek to maintain a real relationship with Him, always standing on His Word and seeking to bring our family together in the love and fellowship of Christ. We also seek to meet people where they are, to not be judgmental and to pray that they get to know Christ for themselves. The first requirement is that we love them with the love of the Lord and realize that He knows them better than we do, and that He does not desire that they be lost. Currently, some of my grandchildren are actively involved in church. We continue to pray for each of them to know Jesus Christ personally and to live for Him so that they can know the Joy and Peace that come from Him alone.

Is It I?
Brittnay Harrell-Stanley

On Sunday, April 22, 2018, I sat in Sunday School and listened to the lesson being taught. I posed a question to my pastor: "Why is it that when I minister to others, they seem to always have a reason or excuse to not come to church? What should I do?" He challenged me to look within myself and ask myself: "Am I the reason I do not produce any fruit?" After thinking about what he asked me to do, I began to ask myself the hard questions: Is my effort to win souls for Christ being out-shadowed by my hypocrisy? My answer to that is YES. I am the biggest hypocrite and sinner I know. I am a sinner who fell and got up by the *grace* and *mercy* of the Lord. I have been focused on the Lord, but I am guilty of taking my eyes off the Lord; every time I do, others see me be a hypocrite. They saw me being mean, rude, hateful, disrespectful, unforgiving, judgmental, and unfaithful. I have discounted God and His blessings on my life. I defiled my body with a substance, I cursed, and I have been quick to condemn others.

The Lord has given me the gift of awareness, boldness, and the desire to reach others in their season of hurting. I strive to be as transparent as ever. In John 21:17, Jesus asked Peter the third time if he loved Him. Peter answered *"Lord, You know all things; You know that I love You."* I have entered a season of hurt and pain as a test of my faith. The first time I rededicated my life back to Christ I believed Christ asked me the same question He asked Peter, but I could not hear him because I was still in the world and trying to follow Christ. I was lukewarm in my faith. The second time I desired to get baptized, the Lord saw I needed to right my wrongs with my fellow brothers and sisters in Christ. The third time I desired to get baptized, I lost my job. My husband and I were lost and confused. While preparing for my baptism, I gained a faith so strong with my Savior, I was beginning to understand the Word. I saw things with my spiritual eyes that I never saw before—I had acquired the spiritual gift of discernment. One night while preparing for bed, I talked to the Lord. He responded very clearly: "Do you love me?" I answered, "Yes. I want to follow you, Lord, but what do I do with my husband? I desire to respect him. However, it would be difficult with him in my ear, telling me to not worry about him." I gave him back to Christ and began my journey of this new life. I was like Peter; I had little faith. I was worried about everybody around me except the one who could change my situation—the Lord God Almighty, who is, was, and is to come.

I am the worst sinner I know. I have led others away from the Lord unconsciously. For a gay friend's birthday, I purchased a rainbow cake. In the LBGTQ community, rainbow represents their sexuality. However, to me, a rainbow represents the promise God gave us that He will not flood the world again with water, but I failed to minister to her what the *rainbow* represents to Christians. Unfortunately, she did not accept Christ because I did not use the opportunity to represent Him. Instead of winning a soul for Christ, I lost a soul. I have reached out to her and have apologized for not loving her correctly and have asked if I could pray for her. She refused but stated she did not believe I encouraged her sin. Even though she refused prayer, I said a prayer for her before going to bed and will continue to do so.

Regarding my husband, I pushed him away from Christ by not being approachable and patient. I am judgmental and am losing faith in him going to the cross with his life. However, I am determined to continue ministering to him and praying for him because I know the power of prayer; the prayers of my earthly family and church family saved my life!

The poem that follows is a unique testimony. Marriage is honorable in the sight of God and was ordained by Him. God gave man a special place in the family—to lead and to love his wife. Romans 3:23 states: *"For all have sinned and fall short of the glory of God."* In mending relationships that have been broken as a result of falling short of God's glory, we are reminded to repent to God and to ask forgiveness from those we have hurt. This poetic testimony was written from the heart of Zachary Stanley and dedicated to wives.

The Best Husband You Never Had
(For Wives)

My intentions are to be the husband you never had ...
The opposite of the Old me, that caused you to
Be disappointed or sad.
To be the best me that I can possibly be ...
So that I can love you like you've never been
Loved and give you all of me.

Now I know I haven't been the best man ...
I can possibly be, but please understand
I'm doing my best, I want nothing less
Than the best for you, Cause I love you,
I really do love you.

I could never take back the things I've
Done or the things I've said ...
But what I can do, what I wanna do
Is be that husband you never had.

I'll be your protector, I'll work hard to provide ...
I'll be your help meet, your ride or die.
Giving me your heart will not be in vain ...
Show me your love and I'll do the same.

It's important to me to be your best friend first ...
To treat you and love you like Jesus did the church.
I've made my mistakes ...
I know I haven't been awake
To your needs and desires
But now I'm on fire.
To give you what you need to be a better husband indeed.

Trust and believe that 1ˢᵗ is God's place ...
Cause I know if we trust in Him, He will make a way.
God will bring us together, stronger than ever.
All we have to do is let go, and He'll bless us with his favor.

There is no room for God and pride ...
So let's get rid of our pride, cause God is on our side.
My mission is to make you happy, keep you happy, and
never ever make you sad ...
I'll be your best friend, your soul-mate
Your lover and more than anything ...
The best Husband you never had.

I love you!

Revelations
Timothy Q. Cochran

My name is Timothy Q. Cochran. I am a 35-year old Black male, born and reared in Atlanta, Georgia. I am a graduate of Frederick Douglass High School in Atlanta, Georgia, where I graduated with honors. While in high school, I played football for the Douglass Astros. One thing I loved about playing football was learning to recite the model prayer after every practice and every game. The prayer brought us together as a team and family and through some tough times, including the death of teammates and classmates. While in high school, I was a student in Morris Brown College's *Upward Bound Program.* I am also a graduate of Jackson State University in Jackson, Mississippi, where I received the Bachelor of Arts degree in Computer Science. At the age of 12, I was saved. However, I was not fully committed through the years.

I lived a moral life with values that were instilled in me by my family. Every time I left home going to school, work, or anywhere, my grandmother always said to me: "Keep God first in any and everything that you do," and that is how I have lived my life. I have never been arrested, and I do not have kids everywhere. My walk with Jesus Christ has been amazing. I have truly been blessed and I give all thanks to our Lord and Savior. I have had some rough and hard times, but God has seen me through. Being a young Black man, I am here to tell all young people that God can see you through. There will be some hard times. However, the tough times will make you stronger, and God will be there to see you through.

I have had my *Patmos Island* experience and have experienced the Lord speaking to me. In September of 2012, I moved from Jackson, Mississippi to Warner Robins, Georgia, where I was in a promising relationship that went bad very quickly. (I was not always consistent in my walk with Jesus Christ. In April of 2013, I moved into my own place, which I consider my *Patmos Island* and started visiting a church located near my home. A few months later, I joined the church. I have lived in the house five years and have continued my walk with Jesus Christ. Within that time, I had some heartaches, but I remained faithful in my walk with Jesus Christ. I prayed and talked to God in my walk, and He always told me to stay patient and humble. I obeyed, and I went from moving to Middle Georgia and having nothing, to being blessed with a roof over my head; from working two jobs, to working one job. I also found a new church home and a new family-to-be! God has truly blessed me, and He can bless you. Know that God is not a genie in a bottle; He is our King, Lord, and Savior. We must stay consistent and faithful in our walk with God. *Try God—Try Jesus Christ!!!*

Living for Likes
Aneitra Stephens

In my own personal dealing with Generation Z, I have noticed that they accept Jesus as their Savior but not their Lord. They refuse to submit to Jesus and His will. They do not have faith in anyone. They only have faith in things and are only moved by material things. Teaching that the understanding of faith and learning to submit to His will is vital. There are so many belief systems operating on the premise that it is not logical to believe in things that one cannot see, or that Jesus is not who He says He is. We must help Generation Z to realize this thought process is a trick of the enemy. We must also encourage them to not use their God-given energy in attempting to determine if a conspiracy exists to get young people, especially of African descent, to believe in the Jesus displayed in pictures. Doing so would be submitting to another trick of the enemy. They must stop falling for the tricks of the enemy. Matthew, Chapter 4 states that Satan tested Jesus in the desert three times. Belief in Jesus was never meant to be taken literally. Belief is having faith. Faith is believing in something you cannot see. Jesus came here to show us that His belief in His father was by faith, even when He did not understand what God was doing. Our faith should be the same way.

To make it personal: At the lowest point in my life, I did not know scripture by heart. I was not going to church on a regular basis; I was not even praying for myself. God still brought me out of the darkness. It was then that He gave me another chance to live for Him. It was through Him that I was saved. I realized that He did not have to do it, but He did. *None* of my *friends* and the people that gave me all the *likes and shares* were there for me. They were there to talk about me and speculate, but *JESUS* was and is always there.

The things I had acquired while I was *living for likes* did not mean a thing if it meant embarrassing myself and my family, if it cost me my freedom, or if it meant I had to have my child in prison. Material things are trendy and describe the belief system of

Generation X. I have observed, via social media interactions, that many are *living for likes.* Those who post information that used to be considered *taboo* are considered *trending* or *sharing.* Trends, likes, or shares will be the downfall of this generation because they do not think about the consequences of their actions. They will be parents one day and have parents and family that will be affected by the poor decisions from *shares and likes,* because their postings on social media can be searched on Google for years to come. The things they do and say on social media can affect the college they attend and the careers they may choose in the future. I believe the only reason it is so prominent is because of the platform. The trends will fade away. They will die down because they have no doctrine to support their beliefs. If they had a doctrine to support their beliefs, they would be as bored as they are with everything else.

Some people will not put forth the effort to learn for themselves. As a Millennial interacting with Generation Z, I can see that people will continue to be lost if they continue to seek approval from their unequal peers. Christians should not seek approval from non-Christians. If you believe that Jesus died for you, and He did, you would speak up for the Kingdom and not let others lead you astray.

Words to Live by On This Journey Called Life

Ola Finney
The fear of the Lord *is to hate evil;*
Pride and arrogance and the evil way
And the perverse mouth I hate.

Proverbs 8:13

Whatever catastrophe occurs in your life, have faith. The Lord is bigger than all problems. Take it to the Lord and leave it at His feet. I pray every day, thanking Jesus for walking with me in the journey called life. I am thankful for the long life, wisdom, and grace He has given me. You can be blessed the same—and even more—if you have faith and let Him lead you in this journey called life.

The testimonials that follow were submitted by the children of The Link Baptist Church. They are very inspirational. It is evident that some children are attending church and are learning about our Lord, Jesus Christ. Their letters and notes reveal that the Lord is still on the throne and at work.

①

Truth

Dear Lord I am very glad that
you gave Me life thank you for

holding Me in your life it sombody
is in the Darkness pull them
out please pull the out of the
Darkness.

Be sure to know that you sins will
find you out we have a cruel
world so when you get up
with god you should say no more
devil alot more god

②

self denial (vs. 6) Renouncing
all things for chrisj's sake, retraining
everything. self satifaction (vs. 6)
better is a little with righteousn
ess, than vast revenuses without
justist. Justice

God I love you very much
and I hope and praise for
the girl alea that came to
our church and the one that
was crying and I pray for
every day and I hope she
get better for her soal and
I hope I see her again at
church.

Trinity Carter   6-10-18   ③

God gave us Glory, Peace, Faith

honesly is the
best Policy

God

Jesus   holy
              spirit

Know more
no more   Some People
                         have
              Faith   narcissism

they will find a way to
make it about them

narcissism—bad

SUMMARY AND CONCLUSION

It is a fact that multiracial congregations cannot survive without strong leaders who are completely certain that culturally and racially diverse congregations are in God's plan. To lead the congregation into unity, church leaders must have multicultural and interracial lifestyles. They must have a passion for building the church as God has commanded. They must relay the message, the passion and the commitment to their church membership. In doing so, they must also maintain a proper balance between the purpose and reason for the church's existence-to honor and worship the Lord and Savior, Jesus Christ, and to fulfill the Great Commission. To maintain this balance, church leaders must pray for God to lead them in selecting new leaders who possess the qualities necessary to serve the present age and who are willing to step up to the plate to accomplish desired results. Church leaders must also pray for guidance in motivating and empowering the new leaders to serve.

Establishing or building a multicultural church is a very challenging experience, but it is an accomplishable task. God never gives His followers a task that they cannot do; He prepares and leads them in accomplishing it. He would not have included the Great Commission as a command to evangelize if the task was too great. In simple terms, God allowed the gospel writers to tell His *church* where they are to go, what they are to do, and who they are to reach. This is outlined in what is called *The Great Commission,* which certainly requires church leaders to establish a church that reaches across racial lines.

Another challenge in building the multicultural church is dealing with church members who reject the multicultural concept. It is significant to note that when congregations become diverse, anxiety increases, and attitudes of prejudice and tension are not likely to disappear. What usually happens is that both attitudes surface more. In fact, some people do not realize their prejudices until they are placed in a multicultural setting, especially if they feel it was forced on them. Pastors must ensure that opponents of the multicultural concept—especially their members—are made aware of the deep-rooted message in the Great Commission. The Kingdom of God must be multicultural because God is the creator of multiethnicity.

Yep states:

> Being multiethnic is more meaningful than just being bicultural. It is also more difficult. It involves interacting with people of many different cultures. There are many expressions of Latino/Hispanic, Black/African American, and Asian American cultures, as well as many variations of white/European culture. You may be able to understand and embrace one culture that's different from your own, but embracing multiethnicity, although it is much harder, is also more reflective of the Kingdom.

Every person in the world is important to God. Each person has been created in God's image-regardless of the gender, skin color, sexual orientation, physical or mental ability, or culture. We are members of one body in Christ and none of us is a foreigner or an outsider to Jesus. We belong to the same human family, and Jesus is the one who unites us. This being the case, there is no reason why all churches should not embrace multiculturalism.

Establishing a multicultural church is somewhat of a slow

and steady process. Traditionalism in the church, while being a stabilizing influence in times of transition and trouble can also be a source of death to kingdom work. Traditionalism in Black and White churches have guarded the continual handing down of doctrine and has created a solid cultural foundation over much of the history of America. It has also helped create a stable church for the purposes of evangelism. However, in this present generation, tradition has become a stumbling block to reaching out in increasingly mixed ethnic nation. The present culture is much different from that of 80 years ago, and the world itself is vastly different.

Prayer is paramount in building a multicultural church. Bowling-Dyer states:

> Organizations must first commit to regular prayer regarding multi-ethnicity. Multi-ethnicity is not just a trendy policy; it is the manifestation of a scriptural value that is countercultural. Those who commit to multi-ethnicity will be dealing with issues on different physical and spiritual levels, and they will need the power of the resurrected Jesus to bring things together.

Talk is cheap when it comes to church leaders saying they are dedicated to building a multicultural church. Crespo states:

> It is critical for organizations to not only say they are committed to multi-ethnicity, but to demonstrate that commitment through structural changes. Even if it's just small baby steps. At some point an organization needs to make these changes, and even small changes can help to bring bigger changes later.

Only with a high value for reconciliation can a multicultural church be established or a traditional church be converted into a multicultural church. Lundgren states:

> You can't do multiethnicity unless you have a high value for reconciliation. You have to be willing as an organization to go back in your history and deal with areas where people have been hurt by the organization or by other people in the organization— White people on White people, Black on Black, whatever the case.

Pastors and church leaders must understand and explain to lay people that a degree of risk is evident in building a multicultural church. The risk is by no means reason enough to stop pursuing the goal. It must be understood that it is attainable and must be obtained to be aligned with the Word of God. It is important to note that there will be those in the membership who must be confronted and helped to work through their racist attitudes and prejudices.

In determining the physical and spiritual needs, interests, customs, and desires of those residing in the church community, church leaders who are truly attempting to grow their church and embrace multiculturalism provide training to the laity in evangelism. They also utilize focus groups to analyze research and provide feedback. This knowledge serves as an aid in designing or redesigning the entire worship service—whichever is needed—to attract prospective members.

Since more people attend worship service than any other church activity, church leaders seeking to build a multicultural church must put a lot of time and effort in worship design. Because of the varied cultures, they must select a target group then proceed to focus on the desires of the group in terms of the worship experience. They must understand that the physical surroundings are important and must ensure that they are appealing.

Not only must church leaders understand the importance of

the physical surroundings to prospective members, they must also understand that people want top notch quality in every aspect of their worship experience. They want the atmosphere to be pleasing, and they expect to both be welcomed and feel welcomed.

Balance is everything. In all areas of Kingdom work: evangelism, worship, fellowship, discipleship, and ministry, there must be balance. It can be created in a variety of ways to ensure equity. In seeking to understand the desires of prospective members who are members of varied cultures, church leaders must take into consideration their choice of music. Once it is determined, they must design or redesign the worship experience to include a variety of music. Variety, in general, is what church leaders must provide if they expect to attract people from varied cultures. The variety can be broad and must also include the time scheduled for worship. Some cultures prefer early worship; others prefer midmorning or evening worship. Therefore, church leaders must consider the desires of their target group. They must realize that they cannot cater to every person who lives in the church community, but they can, however, make every person who enters the church doors feel welcomed and extend an invitation to discipleship and fellowship. The main thing church leaders must remember is that the desires and interests of the target group must remain the primary focus.

To make a positive impact for our Lord Jesus Christ, we, the church, must be willing to accept the fact that we have not gotten it right. We must be willing to admit the error of our ways, and maybe then, the millennial generation will listen to and seek God's message. As evident in the vision and mission statements below, The Link Baptist Church was established with this principle at the forefront. It is, however, a work in progress.

Vision Scripture

After these things I looked, and behold, a great multitude which no one could number, of all nations, tribes, peoples, and tongues, standing before the throne and before the Lamb, clothed with white robes, with palm branches in their hands, and crying out with a loud voice, saying, "Salvation belongs to our God who sits on the throne, and to the Lamb!"
Revelations 7:9-10

Vision

To be a contemporary church that will exalt the name of Jesus Christ by exalting and encouraging the kingdom of God in this new generation and multicultural world.

Mission

Following Jesus and building the kingdom of God in today's changing world. We work to make these a part of all we do.

- Dependency on God
- Honesty in all things
- Relationships that are real
- Diversity in the body
- Relevance in the culture
- Empowerment in the believer

Core Values

Core values are what we feel God highly values for the Link Baptist Church.

Multicultural

Macon is a city that is quickly growing in its number of internationals, and it certainly has a very culturally diverse population. People mix through the workplace, education and in other areas as well. This is especially true of the younger generations. We expect it in the world and feel the church is learning to expect it in the church. We have found a richness in incorporating multiculturalism, and we feel God has created us to recognize and enjoy the power and fellowship in the unity of believers.

Contemporary

Music plays an important part in expressing our worship and service to God. The Link Baptist Church uses music from today to help people meet and talk with Him. However, the contemporary aspect is not just important in music. It is important in matters of style and organization and in the way of doing church as well. The Link Baptist Church gets to the issues and addresses what God is saying to the issues of today. It is also a church where people can make a difference in this world by finding—through God—a place to work for Him and help other people.

Hope

Powerful and encouraging examples of *hope* in this world exist. Social media, wars, racism, politics, bigotry, etc. have taken over almost every part of our lives. We must always seek *hope*. This book was designed to give encouragement to the world and to build the Kingdom of God. Thus, we, as Christians, must keep plowing, pressing, and praying. We must not be ashamed of the *hope* that we have in the return of Jesus Christ. John 14:2-3 states:

> *In My Father's house are many mansions; if it were not so, I would have told you. I go to prepare a place for you. And if I go and prepare a place for you, I will come again and receive you to Myself; that where I am, there you may be also.*

Some believers have fainted and fallen during some difficult times, but all is not lost. Please be encouraged to get back on the battlefield for The Lord. Brothers and sisters, please be encouraged to get back up again and depend on the grace of God in Jesus. It appears that so many are tired and weary. Again, be encouraged, as we pray for one another and fight the good fight of faith.

We, as Christians, must not only live in the future, we must view our lives in the future tense. It is our heartfelt prayer that we be encouraged as we encourage one another that it will be very much worth it in the end. The Bible oftentimes reminds us to keep our minds focused upward on the cross of Jesus Christ. I promise you, it will be worth it. I Peter 5:10 states: *"But may the God of all grace, who called us to His eternal glory by Christ Jesus, after you have suffered a while, perfect, establish, strengthen, and settle you."*

We, as believers, know what it is like to have a spiritual mindset—that we, now more than ever, understand the goodness and kindness of our Savior, Jesus Christ. In the end, our prayer is that Jesus be lifted, and we know that *He* will do the *drawing, changing,* and *saving.* Be encouraged, my fellow workers, to keep the faith and trust that Jesus will strengthen all of us during our difficult times and days. Much love to you and may our Lord—Jesus Christ—richly bless and keep you.

Until Jesus returns,
Pastor Kenneth McMillan

Therefore gird up the loins of your mind, be sober, and rest your hope fully upon the grace that is to be brought to you at the revelation of Jesus Christ, as obedient children, not conforming yourselves to the former lusts, as in your ignorance; but as He who called you is holy, you also be holy in all your conduct, because it is written, Be holy, for I am holy." 1 Peter 1:13-16.

REFERENCES

Barna (2014). *Five trends among the unchurched.* Retrieved from https://www.barna.com/research/ five-trends-among-the-unchurched/#

Barna (2018). *Atheism doubles among Generation Z.* Retrieved from https://www.barna.com/research/ atheism-doubles-among-generation-z/

The Bible. *The Bible study tools.* Retrieved from https://www. biblestudytools.com/ nkjv/james/passage/?q=james+2:14-17

Building Friendships. (2000-2016). *Here's Life Campus Crusade for Christ.* Retrieved from http://www.hereslife.com//prep/ index.htm.

Crespo, O. (2003, Dec.). One Lord, one faith, many ethnicities: How to become a diverse organization and keep your sanity. *Christianity Today.*

Lewis, R., & Wilkins, R. (2002). *The church of irresistible influence.* Colorado Springs: Alive Communications. Grand Rapids, Michigan: Zondervan.

New King James Version. Retrieved from https://www.bible.com.

Lundgren, J. (2003, Dec.). One Lord, one faith, many ethnicities: how to become a diverse organization and keep your sanity, *Christianity Today.*

Stetzer, E. (2003). Planting *new churches in a post modem age.* Nashville: Broadman & Holman, 268.

Stetzer, Ed. (2014). More *thoughts on multicultural church: 3 things to consider about multiculturalism.* Retrieved from https://www.christianitytoday.com/ edstetzer/2014/ may/moving-toward-multicultural-church-3-things-to-consider-abo.html

NOTES

NOTES

NOTES

NOTES

NOTES

Printed in the United States
By Bookmasters